ECHOES FROM THE HEART OF JESUS

A Devotional of Encouragement Through Tough Times

ECHOES
FROM THE
Heart of Jesus

A Devotional of
Encouragement Through Tough Times

BOSEDE SANTOS

A Romans819 (R8:XIX) Ministries Publication,
Published in the United Kingdom
www.romans819.org

Unless otherwise noted, Scripture quotations taken from the New American Standard Bible® (NASB), Copyright © 1960, 1962, 1963, 1968, 1971, 1972, 1973, 1975, 1977, 1995 by The Lockman Foundation Used by permission. www.Lockman.org Scripture quotations marked TPT are from The Passion Translation® (TPT), Copyright © 2017 by BroadStreet Publishing® Group, LLC Used by permission. All rights reserved www.thePassionTranslation.com Scriptures marked AMP are taken from the Amplified® Bible (AMPC), Copyright © 1954, 1958, 1962, 1964, 1965, 1987 by The Lockman Foundation Used by permission. www.Lockman.org Scriptures marked HCSB are taken from the Holman Christian Standard Bible (HCSB): copyright© 1999, 2000, 2002, 2003 by Holman Bible Publishers, Nashville Tennessee. All rights Reserved. Scriptures marked MSG are taken from The Message: The Bible in Contemporary English (TM): copyright©1993, 1994, 1995, 1996, 2000, 2001, 2002. Used by permission of NavPress Publishing Group Scriptures marked ERV are taken from The Easy-To-Read Version (ERV) copyright©2006 by Bible League International Scripture quotations marked (NLT) are taken from the Holy Bible, New Living Translation, copyright ©1996, 2004, 2015 by Tyndale House Foundation. Used by permission of Tyndale House Publishers, a Division of Tyndale House Ministries, Carol Stream, Illinois 60188. All rights reserved.

Paperback ISBN: 979-8-47261-997-4
Hardcover: ISBN: 979-8-48238-603-3

A CIP catalogue record for this title is available from the British Library

Cover Design by R8:XIX Ministries Publications

Typeset by Jotham Communications, Lagos, Nigeria.
Email: jothamoffice@gmail.com Phone: (234) 802 660 3057

First Printing, 2021
Printed and bound in Great Britain by Amazon

What Others Have Said About
Echoes from the Heart of Jesus

To 'finish well' we must overcome all the hardships of life, the most painful being when people we trusted desert us.

Some people learn from these difficulties and move on, but real champions – do more than learn – they invest that experience in others.

Bosede is that kind of champion! She has turned her pain into triumph and wants others to triumph with her. Read! Receive! Overcome! and triumph together.

Dr. Phil Nordin
Chairman, Equip International

Where is God when life is hard? He's closer than you think. *Echoes from the Heart of Jesus* invites you to come thirsty and drink deeply from the ever-replenishing well of God's limitless love. Like cool water on parched ground, each devotional in this book will refresh your spirit, renew your hope, and reignite your passion for the God who knows you by name.

Kim Avery, MA, Business Coach
Author of *The Prayer Powered Entrepreneur: 31 Days to Building Your Business with Less Stress & More Joy*

Echoes from the Heart of Jesus is a creative contribution to enrich the Body of Christ from God's rich tapestry of His people.

Bosede brings the heartfelt prophetic encouragement of a seasoned sojourner. Her texts are selected out of the well-worn causeway of spiritual pilgrims from all generations. In calling the reader deeper in the spiritual life the straight-ahead pithy word pictures are pregnant with fresh revelation.

This devotional work will be inspirational to the casual and seasoned saint alike and assured to be revisited repeatedly and treasured. Delight in the author's largeness of heart and clarity of thought as you read.

Dr. Bryan A Logan.
Senior Leader of Life ConneXion 1992- present

From personal experience in a myriad of desperate times, Bosede shares God's truth to claim and declare in every season. *Echoes from the Heart of Jesus* is a profound combination of scripture and space for reflection through journaling and music.

Discover hope for your spirit and strength for your journey.

Shirley Thiessen, Grief Speaker & Mentor @ Corner Bend Ministries. Author of *The Little Black Funeral Dress: Five Things I Wish Had Known About Grief*

CONTENTS

BONUS CONTENTS

DEDICATION

To everyone who will fight the good fight of faith and not give up, even through the darkest of valleys and the toughest of times, God has pronounced you blessed for your love and endurance, and your trophy is a crown of life – James 1:12.

Keep looking on to Jesus, the Initiator and Refiner of your faith. His plans for you are good and He will bring you to your expected end. You are the manifestation of His glory. Rom.8:19

ACKNOWLEDGMENTS

With gratitude to God for the grace to have stood during days when standing was the only option. Tough as it was, Your Spirit resounded Your promises, which became my fuel day and night.

To my family, thank you for standing firm. We continue to take God at His Word and speak peace to the storms. I will choose your squad any day.

To everyone who in no little way contributed to this book, I am truly thankful.

To all who will pore over the words on these pages, I pray you will be filled with courage and certainty that God is faithful in His love, and a sure Help in times of need.

FOREWORD

Even atheists, at least the ones I know, would welcome, now and then, a direct word from God: something, anything, to let them know that the universe is not a cold and empty place, that someone watches over them, that when they holler, or weep, or whisper, the voice coming back to them is more than their own echo.

And Christians – well, we long for that direct word, especially in times of distress or confusion or sorrow. "Speak, Lord, for your servant is listening." "Jesus, just tell me what to do, and I will do it." "Just tell me where you are and I will be there." And especially this: "Lord, please tell me you love me. Tell me you see what's going on. Tell me you care. Tell me you're with me."

Just one word is all we need. One word that we know, deep in our bones, is more than our own echo.

Bosede Santos gets it. She and her family went through a dark season when, it seemed, everything they had worked a lifetime to build would be lost. In her distress, and confusion, and sorrow, she cried out to God for a way through.

He didn't provide that way through, at least not right away. What He provided was infinitely better: Himself. He showed up. He spoke–not just one word, but a deluge of words, of promises, of affirmations. "I love you. I am with you. I will never leave you. Trust me. Watch me. I will do this. I have got this. I have got you, and all whom you love."

And she knew, in her bones, that the voice she heard was more than her own echo–that the Lord had spoken, from His Word, direct from His heart to hers.

The Lord did sort out, miraculously, her family's distress. But the real prize, the real gift, has been her renewed hope and confidence in the God who sees, and hears, and comes near. The God who speaks, from His heart to hers.

In these pages, Bosede shares this gift. She has soaked long and deep in God's Biblical promises, and meditated long and deep on God's character, and the result is a series of direct words from God's heart to your own.

Read them. Savour them. Trust them. These are not the echoes of your own voice. These are echoes from the heart of Jesus.

Mark Buchanan
Author of *The Rest of God*

PREFACE

"Be strong and courageous, do not be afraid or tremble at them, for the LORD your God is the one who goes with you. He will not fail you or forsake you." Deuteronomy 31:6

"From my distress I called upon the LORD; The LORD answered me and set me in a large place. The LORD is for me; I will not fear; What can man do to me? The LORD is for me among those who help me; Therefore, I will look with satisfaction on those who hate me."
Psalm 118:5-7

Ever been on a roller coaster ride, that left you reeling? The kind you got on and wished you had not once it started? Especially if you are not one to get pumped on an overdose of adrenaline coursing through your veins. Being logged forcibly along sharp twists and turns and upside-down loops. Your stomach completely snarled, heart in mouth, fingers frozen, you want it to stop. Frantic, you want to get off. Even for those who get excitement from such rush, it would be an overkill. I have. It was a chair o' plane adventure gone awry! I prayed hard till I got off!

F.A.C.T. Life can at times present like such undesirable rollercoaster rides, and sadly, not even one of us is immune from such topsy-turvies called life challenges. These challenges we experience could parallel what I consider a pesky mutation. One where what I call the 'life gene', once characterized by peace, as God ordered, sneakily morphs into a disturbing deviant, chockfull of disappointments, sorrows and losses or breakdowns in diverse forms. Like cancer, it can metastasize rapidly and ambush one. A morbid picture right!

Certainly, never a season to relish. But dare I say, can be most transformational in someone's life. If allowed, God can guide our lives to His desired destination for us as we return the 'reigns' (*my poetic licence play on words*) to Him. Hebrews 12:7,8.

These times can be as fleeting as they are long drawn. More often as well, this is the period when God seems far away, His voice silent and drowned out by the clang of the challenges. Hearts cry out, "Lord, speak to me." "Say anything!" "I want to hear Your voice."

Rest assured, through these raging and troublesome times, Jesus is always there in your heaving and rolling boat. His guarantee is to be present with us always, and His Holy Spirit resounds those time-tested promises which anchor our hearts to His unfailing love. With these promises, we can 'make war', and fight our way through the slog! 1Timothy1:18,19.

Through seasons when my family and I have had to walk the tightrope of such unnerving and tear-jerking trials, God remained infinitely faithful. His assurances became our balancing pole; they kept us steady and moving forward. Steadying us to withstand these undesirable forces and helping to centre us back to where we progressed towards our victory.

The Holy Spirit, swaddling our souls with these promises, shielding us from the storm the enemy was welling up all around us. He constantly reminded us of scriptures, and our hearts stayed strong. The more of His words we held on to, the firmer our footing walking through the situations.

The words I share in *Echoes from the Heart of Jesus* were born of similar reassurances I received as my heart throbbed to the echo of those promises. In the deafening din and ache of those situations, Jesus' voice broke through, calm, steady and quiet, uttering assuring relief through His words of comfort. The ensuing peace was (*always is*) nothing we could have faked.

During those periods, as a family, we had a choice to make, stagger through the storm or steadfastly follow on in faith. Tough and trying as it was, we opted to follow in faith. Our choice made the difference between walking in victory and suffering a black and blue defeat at the hand of the enemy. We elected to persevere even when the circumstances were dealing our confidence deathly blows. The gutsy grit through the storm is the fight of faith spoken of in 1Timothy 6:12. Cliché as it may be, the battleground remains the mind; the place to take the enemy captive.

Through spells of testing, the distress makes Jesus' voice seem distant and difficult to hear or even decipher amidst the jangle. *Echoes from the Heart of Jesus* is offered as the sword of offence with which to push back on the advancing intimidations of the enemy.

Jesus assures us as we remain submitted to Him and keep resisting the devil, that he'll pretty much scuttle off in terror with his tail in between his legs. (James 4:7)

Jesus threw him off repeatedly by asserting the word of God. God's promises become the rivers of living waters, which will gush out of your heart, bringing a torrent of deliverance in those situations, and trust me, devils can't survive in water; they can't swim! –Matthew 8:32, Luke 11:24. Drown Satan out with the truth of God's word!

My desire, and prayer, is to see you immersed in these promises, and catch the beating of Jesus' heart echoing these promises made over two thousand years ago. They are true, and full of life and power for victory still. God's plan also remains abundant overflowing life for you–John. 10:10.

I pray this will lead you to a place of rest where you can clearly discern the Master's voice. Despite your situation, grasp His life-giving word set to carry you on to your victory.

Resolve not to recoil at the enemy's yelp; sincerely, it's all it is. The One whose Word you wield, and who lives right inside you is the Lion of the Tribe of Judah!

Let him roar in you and through you. You are a VICTOR!!

For His Glory,
Bosede
Rom. 8:19

INTRODUCTION

"For as the rain and the snow come down from heaven, and do not return there without watering the earth and making it bear and sprout, and furnishing seed to the sower and bread to the eater; So will My word be which goes forth from My mouth; It will not return to Me empty, without accomplishing what I desire, and without succeeding in the matter for which I sent it."
Is. 55:10,11.

*E*choes From the Heart of Jesus came to be from an encounter with God, one night. I was seeking direction for my family as we soldiered through the dark trenches of a financial challenge. We trusted God with every breath to meet our obligations. Craved words of instruction to get us out of that dugout.

I had hoped for a direct word that night; same as the disciples received when Jesus met them at the Sea of Tiberias after His resurrection, having toiled through the night and caught nothing. At dawn, when He met them at the shore, He instructed them to cast their net to the right side of the boat. Scripture records, they obeyed and could not haul in the many fish they caught. John. 21:1-9.

My plea was for such grace. To receive the same directive and victorious word that would change our lives. No such instruction came my way but tested promises from His Word streamed through my mind. I flipped my Bible to promises, which proved true for us, and other Christians, through the years.

As I pored over these words, did my heart dance with encouragement! They yanked off the shroud of despair that had covered it until then. My heart nestled. Free at last, from the turmoil and fear that had been raging inside me.

There was an unmistakable presence within me. His encouragements hit the bull's eye of my heart as He sat with me in the stillness of that night. Exposed to the light of His word, the gloom and doom image in my mind got the marching order.

The glorious light of hope and victory dawned in my heart. Without a doubt, His word did not return to Him empty. No 'hocus-pocus', 'abracadabra' act, just His love flowing through me. The compassion in His voice, as He spoke, swaddled my heart, gave me the trust I needed to believe His every utterance. My thoughts of our predicament shifted.

God needed to get my heart to a place of hope and full reliance on His word. No quick fix. His words encircled my heart, transition from my head into my heart, transforming my perception and words. I 'saw' the promises. His words about the issues became my words. Grabbing on to His promises to take care of things. I can report that help came from undreamed of sources. He took care of things! At last, those direct words of instruction followed. He led us through in triumph!

Amidst the angst, thoughts tore at my heart of others who could be dealing with such a dilemma. I wondered how they were managing under the circumstances. My eagerness to share what had transformed my condition and brought me comfort heightened, hence *Echoes from the Heart of Jesus*.

I desired to offer a hand the same way Jesus reached for me. Take words from Jesus' heart to theirs; hopeful words that will move them to look to the One mighty to deliver. Reassuring words of Jesus' nearness, just a breath away. Words that will lasso them to His side and help them hear His voice above the clamour of the storm; reminding them of how much He loves them. Words, true and tried, sure to keep them strong through the fight.

Echoes from the Heart of Jesus is an invitation into such depth of relationship that will cause you to abide, draw from and dig your roots deep into the only One able to deliver and give victory from every dare and snare of the devil.

How to get the most out of *Echoes From The Heart of Jesus*

I divided the devotional into thirty days. Each day begins with a scripture, followed by words of encouragement streaming from the lips of Jesus to you. I presented this section how I heard Jesus speak during those troubled times. Envision Him as the Psalmist did, sitting by your right hand, speaking these words of life and assurance to you each day.

May I assure you; these words are not frivolous or random. I believe these are words that, by His Spirit, He wants to speak to you today.

Each day ends with a **call to action**, (📖) a response from you. I understand that information without a follow-up action amounts to a waste of time-the Bible describes it as deceiving oneself. James.1:22-25.

Think through what you have heard using the Journal page; ponder and write your thoughts as you mull over these questions and scriptures. Connect with them and allow the Holy Spirit to chat with you and shed His light on your heart. Let Him arm you for your victory as He uncovers the secrets in those verses. These entries will serve as a memorial of what God is doing for you. One day you will read over, or even share them with your family and friends, to bear witness to the goodness of God. There is something in writing that brings clarity, direction, and calm to an otherwise blustery predicament.

I included suggested **hymns** or **worship songs** (🙌), so you can seize the opportunity of this time in His presence to worship. Never mind, even if these are not your typical style or choice of worship songs, listen to the lyrics of the songs. I chose them on purpose to bolster and inspire you to connect with and expect what God will do. Worshipping is hard during these times. Worship the most, regardless. Worship gets the Father's attention and lifts His hand to act on your behalf. Psalm 22.

Though a 30-day devotional, please read as many portions as you need to get your heart rested and fastened on those promises daily. Do this to quieten those noisome babbles contradicting the power in God's words.

Have you noticed how the devil uses that one worn out strategy; challenge the word of God? Remember, faith comes by the continuous hearing of God's words, and more so, through trying times. God has given us His Holy Spirit to empower us.

Be real. When you are tired or feel abandoned, share your heart with Him and ask for His help. He knows anyhow! Desperate and vulnerable? Tell Him. Your cry for His help is your trust in Him.

I beg of you, don't stay defeated. Grab a hold of Him and rise with His grace. Fight despite the fears and doubts! Your joy and peace are His delight–John. 15:11.

I included a bonus section with an extra day's devotional for good measure! Because more than ever, during these times, we need God's wisdom, His word, to skilfully steer through these rock-riddled troubled watercourses, I put in a Bible plan to read through the Psalms and Proverbs within the 31 days.

Included are declarations that will help you create a new reality. The heart and mouth connection will transform your case. Speak out your faith. Speak life into your plight, so don't be silent.

In addition, I added patterns to colour. A psychology and spirituality exist behind those, which I will explain. The loveliness created helps to change your perspective and set your heart up for winning.

I added a playlist to help you always be in the atmosphere of worship. Like you have never done, worship, worship, worship. It always brings God on the scene, lifts your heart, and removes anxiety from you. Please note, I do not own copyrights on any of the songs; they are only suggestions as they helped me to refocus my perception during the hard times. You can buy them on iTunes, Spotify or anywhere else music is sold.

As Paul charged in his letter to the Ephesians, I am as well asking you to stand and keep standing. Use the weapons God made available to you in Christ Jesus-His own armour-the belt of truth, secure around your waist;

righteousness as breastplate protecting your heart; your shield of faith snuffing out any flaming arrow of doubts and lies aimed at you; Gospel of peace sandals securing your feet for your walk of victory and to proclaim His goodness. Your mind, will and emotions protected by your helmet, His salvation. Use your sword of the Spirit, His Word, the truth, that guarantees your freedom to cut through and stab at any opposing force; lay to rest any lie or accusation of the devil. God has equipped you for the offensive!

If we need these weapons to keep standing, even after we have done the things to stand, that shows the courage we need to muster during these seasons. When your strength threatens to fail you, God has given you a Helper and Encourager. He is always at hand, cling to Him! He lives right inside you, DO NOT neglect Him.

Two of the scriptures that had a significant impact on me during those hard times were Romans 5 and James 1:2-4. He encourages us to REJOICE in our trials! For real? But understanding that trials build my character–first training me in endurance that develops my grit. Next, strengthening my confident hope that God will deliver me. Resulting in a strong and mature faith. This was huge for me. It was worth the patience. Besides, from the Job narrative, I concluded God knew I could take it and so bragged on me! That cheered and pumped me up somewhat.

The scriptures prompted a radical, fundamental change of my view of challenges. I made sweet lemonade out of the lemons of adversity (My son has a unique spin on this. He says, take out the seeds, plant them, get you an orchard full of lemon trees and prosper at the devil's expense!) Either way, you develop patience, and the devil loses big time! With God's help I played well (and by His grace will keep playing) the hand life circumstances dealt me and won through His power resident in me.

Be assured that as you ride the waves of the journey with courage, focusing on the prize, and cutting through the waves, you will rise above the waves and overcome Satan's opposition. Paddle through with your prayers as if everything depends on it (because they do). Never look back, keep pressing towards God's promises. Endure till you get the promise. Keep your feet planted on the promises, knees bent in prayer, arms loose to offer up sacrifices of praise and release blessings to others, and keep your eyes fixed on Jesus, your prize. Be relentless! Allow God to shape you through it, you will come out a wave rider, trophy of God's grace.

I invite you to embrace the hard seasons, knowing you will win despite the devil's best effort.

Newsflash! There will ALWAYS be hard times, but John 16:33 is our guarantee we will ALWAYS win! Whichever way the victory pans out, we win–Revelation 5.

What I am not saying is for you to settle in these seasons, having a perpetual pity party or developing a martyr complex. Instead, know the truth that *"These trials are only to test your faith, to see whether it is strong and pure. It is being tested as fire tests gold and purifies it—and your faith is far more precious to God than mere gold; so, if your faith remains strong after being tried in the test tube of fiery trials, it will bring you much praise and glory and honor on the day of his return."* 1Peter 1:7. The Living Bible.

Like Job, know for a certainty that, *"He knows every detail of what is happening to me (you); and when he has examined me (you), he will pronounce me (you) completely innocent-as pure as solid gold!"* Job 23:10 (emphasis mine). The Living Bible. You even get gold-plated to the bargain!

Never forget, these times are seasonal, they will pass! What God is interested in, as someone said, is not so much your comfort as your integrity. So go for gold! Let nothing stop you. God built, equipped, and favoured you to outlast and outshine the devil. Start, buff the dullness, sparkle so the on-looking world can see His glory in your life.

Might be you came upon this book by chance and have not yet surrendered your life to the Lordship of Jesus, or maybe you once walked with Him and the troubles of this life have slid you away from Him, I invite you to consider the benefits. He is craning His neck, looking in the distance and calling your name to return home. His arms are wide open, and He will receive you.

At the end, I have included the steps to repentance plus a sample prayer of commitment, symbolic of your decision. Praying this prayer alone will not make you a Christian. As you repent and invite Jesus into your life, for the first time, or in rededication, despite life's tugs and pulls, daily committing to this lifelong relationship, a makeover that only God's Holy Spirit can start will begin in your heart.

Remember this, though you walk, T.H.R.O.U.G.H, through the valley of the shadow of death, you must fear no evil because His rod of protection and staff of support and leadership are present to bring you comfort. Ron Kenoly's song says it well, *"if you catch hell don't hold it, if you're going through hell, don't stop...."* When He has brought you through, He will, with great joy and delight in you not giving up, set out a lavish banquet for you, to the humiliation of your gloaters-Satan and his cohorts. Psalm 23.

This is not forever; you are passing through, coming out to a fiesta!

I AM WITH YOU

"These things I have spoken to you, so that in Me you may have peace. In the world you have tribulation, but take courage; I have overcome the world." John 16:33

Good morning my lovely one. Today, my word for you is, "it is a new day! A day to rejoice and be glad." Will you choose this with me? I am always here.

What you are going through will not swamp you if you will believe me. I promised you I already conquered the world. I gave myself so you can win every time the enemy tries to assault you. My peace is lasting and will keep your heart from fainting.

One thing you can always count on, when I say it, I mean it and therefore will bring it to pass. I have honoured my word above my name and therefore bound by what my mouth utters. I am set to do you good because your joy matters to me. Your wellbeing is my priority.

I said you are more valuable than the birds of the air and the flowers of the fields which outshine Solomon in his fullest splendour. If I will take care of these, will I not care for you?

You are my treasure, my prized possession. I know every part of you-your thoughts, even before you think them, your emotions, which you must learn to master, and every path your feet will take or have taken to get here.

To have numbered every strand of hair on your head shows how much I cherish you. Fix your gaze on me, so the raging winds and waves won't rock you and make you doubt my love for you and goodness towards you.

I have not left you without help. My Holy Spirit is in you and with you always, to help you accomplish every task and bring you through triumphantly.

The thoughts of your heart may scream trouble, but my words will forever speak peace. My words speak life. My words speak hope. My promise to you remains and will not fail you. I cannot lie.

Even when all around you do not line up with my word, choose to believe me. It is easy to believe in me because of what you have seen or heard others experience through my word, but you must choose to believe me for yourself today. What will you believe my word for today?

I prayed for you to abide and be one with the Father as He and I are one. So, settle this in your heart once and for all, I will never leave you, neither will I ever abandon you. Though you do not see or feel I am there, I am. Rest in the constancy of my love for you.

You are very precious to me, and I delight not only in doing things for you but seeing you full of joy. I want to show you how to walk through this coming out in victory. I will walk every step of this journey with you. I never leave a sheep behind, but I guide every one of them to the verdant pasture where they will find rest and renewal.

My Active Response

- What will I choose, what I see or what He says?
- Read Matthew 8:5-13; Luke 7:1-9.

My Worship

- "Breathe" - Michael W. Smith
- "Standing on the Promises" - Selah

Jesus has left his peace with me. (His sure word) so in him I have confidence. That it is possible to win in the battles of life because he did. He has walked the Path ⇒ He is my high priest who knows every infirmity and trial I can face and he has won them all.

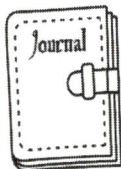

Journal

REJOICE IN ME

*Those who love Your law have great peace,
and nothing causes them to stumble.*
Psalm 119:165

My child, do you trust my commitment to you? I was sent to die for you. I could have backed out for fear of losing out, but I did not. I held my part of the deal. I went all the way for you.

Remember, the only time I was hindered to do good was because of unbelief. Unbelief is not just doubting me or my word, it is believing another's lie that I cannot or am unwilling to help you.

My word is my bond, and that is what I am giving you today, to assure your peace. My ears are open to your cry, I notice your tears, I mark your sighs and I am working things out. Things might appear delayed, but I already said there is an appointed time for everything under the heaven.

I instructed you to store my word in your heart and keep my word in your mouth; be consistent in thinking and speaking it. Then, the things I have said will catch your attention, and they will bring you prosperity and success in all you do.

There is a sure outcome for every act of faith, but you must rise with courage and rejoice though you have not yet seen the promise. My hand is ready to hold you and help you. Never get discouraged.

You will face many challenges because you have agreed to follow my will, but hold steady, I have promised to deliver you from every one of them. No one who trusts in me will be put to shame. I promise to you today, though the young lion experiences lack and go hungry, everyone who seeks me will not be deprived of any good thing.

Cheer up! My presence in your life is your haven – your safe and secure place where the uproars of life will not harm you. They may rage, they will rage, but be confident that I will never leave neither will I forsake you. My Spirit is the Greater One within you, guiding your every step, instructing your heart so you will not falter. My angels are all around you, protecting you from harm and disasters. So, rejoice!

Do not give in to worry; it displeases me and changes nothing. You know now, faith in me, faith in my word is what pleases me and moves me to act on your behalf. Worry only steals your peace and makes you doubt me and my plans for your life.

I made you a promise and will not go back on my word; my plans are for your wellbeing, I will never hurt you, and I will bring you to your imagined good end, which could never match what I have planned. I always go over and above your expectations. I am working out the wonderful future I wrote about and already spoke into being for you

My Active Response

- What is my proclamation of faith? Search for scriptures promising my solution and meditate on them till I 'see' the promises.
- Read Daniel 3; Luke 8:40-48.

My Worship

- "My Life is in Your Hands" - Kathy Troccoli
- "Lord I Believe in You" - Brooklyn Tabernacle Choir

_____

_____

_____

_____

_____

_____

_____

_____

_____

_____

_____

_____

_____

_____

_____

_____

Journal

_____

_____

THE JOY OF ASKING

So I say to you, ask, and it will be given to you; seek, and you will find; knock, and it will be opened to you. For everyone who asks, receives; and he who seeks, finds; and to him who knocks, it will be opened. Luke 11:9,10.

Child, I rise with you today to a brand-new day! To walk alongside you, to help you. Know that no part of today will take me by surprise; neither will I be inattentive to help you get through whatever comes as a challenge, nor will I neglect to celebrate your victories. You are one in a million to me!

When the challenges come, remember that I am just a breath away, listening to your request for help. Some things are beyond the reach of your understanding for now, and until I return to take full possession of the earth, the prince of the power of the air is operating in this world. He lives to steal, kill, and destroy, but be confident, I am working out all things for good despite him. Even when things appear distressing and all together confusing, I can use them to your advantage.

I asked you to consider it a great privilege when you must navigate life's rough waters. They mature your character as you brave these dilemmas. You appreciate what stuff you are made of and adjust wherever you need more vigour. I possess the wisdom to steer through these holdups and will not consider it trivial or foolish when you ask me for the wisdom to make it through. I delight in your success.

I promised that whatever you ask the Father in my Name I will do it so our Father may be glorified, and your joy may be full. You must make up your mind though who to believe, the situation, or me.

When you ask me to help, watch out for the double mindedness and be certain that I will act on your behalf. I asked you to make your requests known to me with a thankful heart. Go on, rejoice in the face of these issues, draw the line, and show the devil you know who's in charge; position yourself for victory.

I know it will not always come naturally or easy to rejoice in your troubles, else I would not have pointed it out as the way to go. Don't allow your feelings get the better of you; this is what faith is all about. How would you be if those issues were resolved today? Glad, sad? Then behave in line with your desired end, this is how you attain it. Never get weary of asking me for what you need.

Activate your imagination and see my answers in your heart. Ask the Holy Spirit to help you engage with what the

Father already wrote about your life and start living in the reality of my answer. I will not fail you.

My Active Response
- Who/What will I believe? Learn to practice recounting God's goodness, it sets my face on victory because of His faithfulness
- Read James 1:1-18; Luke 11:5-13.

My Worship
- "Enough" - Jeremy Camp
- "In Jesus' Name" - Darlene Zschech

Journal

Day 4 — I DIED FOR YOU

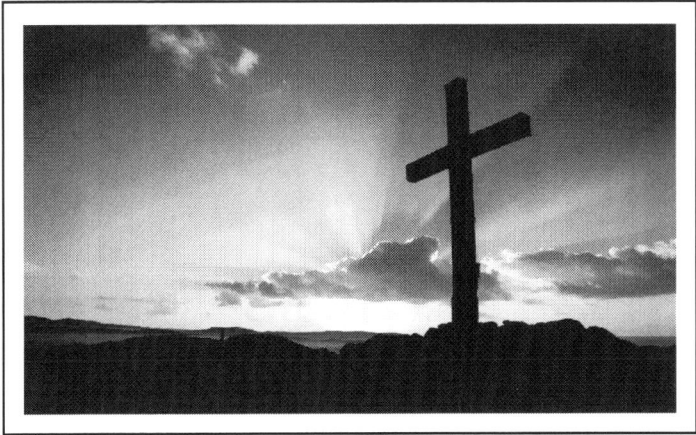

But know that the LORD has set apart the godly man for Himself; The LORD hears when I call to Him. Psalm 4:3

Child, have you considered lately what the gospel is about? Sure, you know it is the good news. But good news about what?

Let me remind you. It is about me offering myself up to pay the price for the sins of the whole world. Our Father wants you delivered from the evil of your present age and restored to His original plan when He created the world. It is your guarantee of the Father's plan to deliver you from the corruption in the world.

Now think about it, if I already died to deliver you from evil, will I still allow you to be subject to it? The god of this world strives to mount pressure on you to cause you to fear what you have already been delivered from. Despite these pressures, you will not be crushed.

When you are bewildered, my wisdom is always available to instruct you and show you what to do. Surely, the tempter will try to bully you, back you into a corner like you have no way out but to believe his lies. I assure you, notwithstanding, I am always with you, and I will defend you. He may slam you down, but you will never be knocked out.

I was tormented and tried, scorned and slayed, all for doing the Father's will. In life, you will also face difficulties because you belong to me. That scoundrel delights in battering you thinking he's getting at our Father; stay courageous, because I overcame in victory, you will too. I live, you will too.

My life will be unmistakably revealed in you as you speak my words deposited in your heart in faith. You were hand-picked for our Father's glory when you put your trust in me and chose to live for Him. He is not about to abandon you now.

Our Father is good to all, and His compassion is towards all He has made. He will always be faithful to His words, and He will extend His infinite grace in all He does.

He is generous towards His own and causes them to be satisfied with good things as He blesses them. He will never abandon the plea of an honest heart. He will take up arms against your assailants and fight on your behalf. He raises up the standard of His word, and like a deluge, it drowns the enemy, who could never survive in the water of the word.

Never let the situation loom larger than your God. What do you think I meant when at the cross I said, "it is finished"? Think about it.

I'm assuring you, there's nothing more left to accomplish where the evil one is concerned. He's been totally vanquished. You can rest in that victory and assert it whatever you are going through. Again I say to you, "it is finished!"

My Active Response
- What else remains when Jesus declared, "it is finished"? Can the enemy negate that?
- Read Psalm 145.

My Worship
- "Your Grace is Amazing (Thank You for What You've Done)" - Greg Sykes
- "You Won't Let Go" - Michael W. Smith

Journal

CELEBRATE ME

He will not fear evil tidings; His heart is steadfast, trusting in the LORD. His heart is upheld, he will not fear, until he looks with satisfaction on his adversaries. Psalm 112:7,8

Good morning, dear child. Today I want us to recap your benefits in me. These are your reasons not to become dispirited. I am reminding you of your status. Victor, and by no means a victim.

When you consider the power of my cross and what my poured-out blood accomplished for you, you will be confident of your position in me, and all I have already apportioned to you.

Our Father said you have been blessed with everything you need to live a goodly and consecrated life by His awesome power. His promises are the surety that you will live the life He had planned for you before the foundation of the earth.

So today, stop awhile and ponder these truths:

- All your sins are forgiven
- All your diseases are healed
- Your life is redeemed from destruction
- You are crowned with loving kindness and tender mercies
- Your mouth is satisfied with good things, restoring your youth like the eagle's
- He performs righteousness and rules in your favour against oppression. He sets you free. He makes His ways known to you
- He gives you His grace and mercy in times of need

That's worth a celebration, don't you think! It's something to shout about from the rooftops. You are such an overcomer!

It is true that the present state of this world is scary, not much room for hope or even faith, but I have asked you to increase your faith. You do this by determining to be upright despite the corruption. You must not be ignorant of my word and the life our Father desires for you. Be informed, don't be aloof in the world, it will guide your prayers.

Yes, you are not of this world, but you are in it to make a difference. Be salt, preserve, flavour this generation; be light, shine the way to me.

Knowledge is power; it will enable you to exercise self-discipline, which will teach you fortitude that stands you in good stead with the Father. God's nature in you equips you to care for others thereby perfecting your love. When you continue to grow this way, you will not be inactive or ineffective in my ways.

These are not the days to fret but chin up! My glory will be seen as you pray my will upon the earth. Will you partner with me?

My Active Response

- Consider the odds; stoop in defeat, or stand in victory. My choice today, dress for the kill in the armour of God; stand in the face of all that beset all around.
- Read Psalm 103.

My Worship

- "Sing and Shout" - Matt Redman
- "Whom Shall I Fear" - Chris Tomlin

Journal

<table>
<tr><td>Day
6</td><td>REST IN MY
FAITHFULNESS</td></tr>
</table>

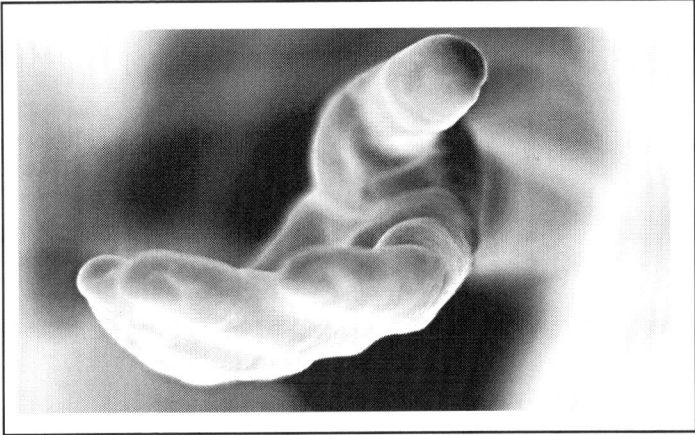

Peace I leave with you; My peace I give to you; not as the world gives do I give to you. Do not let your heart be troubled, nor let it be fearful. John 14:27

Precious one, have you noticed how I use instructions to point your attention to those things our Father abhors? When you follow these instructions, they keep your heart at peace, and you walk in obedience towards God.

Peace, as you know, is not the absence of turmoil, it is just the confident assurance that despite the threatening unrest, I am working things out for your good, and I will not fail you or bring you to shame. This is the kind of peace I give.

I am your Prince of Peace, and my peace will empower you to silence the uproar, so you can rest on the provision of the Father, which promises you wellbeing.

In our Father is all goodness; He will forgive every one of your sins, He will provide mercy and grace, success, and every sense of welfare for times of need. This way, you maintain good health, perform well in every aspect of life because your soul will also be thriving.

This is the covenant I have made with you. I will fulfil my promise no matter how things look. I cannot go back on my words; I have already made the sacrifice. It would be my delight if you commit to this covenant and be strong and sincere with your own part.

For your day, I pronounce my blessing on you. You will be in my care and my face will shine on you continually. I will be a friend to you, and continually look out for you to assure your peace. When your day is over, my promise of sweet sleep is yours to possess because I love you very much.

You have no need to stay awake; your mind working overtime, figuring out solutions to issues that puzzle you. It will only rob you of needed sleep and set you on a futile cycle of irritability and fear.

Rest, and trust our Father who stays on guard looking out for you and commanding His angels to enforce His bid about your situation.

The song I continue to sing over you is one of victory. Will you rest in me today? Will you lay your head on my bosom so you hear my heartbeat and whispers reassuring you all will work out for your good?

I want your joy to be full. Never doubt my commitment to your success in life. The Father delights to display you as the proof of His generosity.

Active Response
- Pause, breathe, and choose to rest in my Father, He is working all things out.
- Read 2Thessalonians 3:1-5.

My Worship
- "It is Well with My Soul" - Horatio Spafford sung by Brian Doerksen
- "Great Are You Lord"-All Sons and Daughters

Journal

THE HOLY SPIRIT,
YOUR HELPER

*May Your lovingkindnesses also come to me, O LORD, Your
salvation according to Your word; so I will have an answer for
him who reproaches me, for I trust in Your word.*
Psalm 119:41, 42

Brother/Sister, I call you so because we are children of the
same Father. As the first born of many siblings, I am glad to
have you as a member of the family.

I also called you friend because I care about you
compassionately and I am attentive to you. I want you to be
secure in our Father's affection for you. Believe it, He dotes
on you! He rejoices over you; He sings over you. He wants
you to find peace in His love for you.

His Holy Spirit is with you as your Helper. He will keep reminding you of my words, what I already spoke to you about the Father. I point your attention to me because the Father is revealed in me. I told you before, every word I uttered was what I heard Him speak. I do not speak of my own whim.

Let's consider some things He already promised. He said He will never condemn you; He has overpowered your enemy. He invites you to the sneak preview of what He will do to those who intimidate you. Get this, He will turn your shame to fame! That sounds like a sweet swap to me.

It keeps getting better, He promised to restore all that was stolen from you. So, what's stopping you from raising your hands in joyful jubilation and being grateful for His salvation? Don't listen to tales or threats. You can trust Him because He always saves completely. Do you believe it?

Have you ever witnessed a rainy day where the ground wasn't soaked; or seeds get watered and not sprout? Until then, His words will always yield a return and never be unfruitful.

May I ask you to declare this over yourself today, "**the Lord is my Helper, I will not fear what man can do to me. I will live to declare the goodness of my God in this land of the living. His love rests on me and makes a way for me.**"

Remind yourself of the miracles you read about in the Bible. They are there to encourage you and build up your faith in me and our Father who promised to raise me up on the third day. Here I am! Is there anything He will deprive you of? Remember also the good you had experienced in the past.

"Count your blessing," the hymn writer says, "name them one-by-one." David urged his soul to bless the Lord and not forget His benefits. Try it out today. Recount my goodness from the past and marvel at how your heart and face will lighten up

I asked you not to get worked up about anything, but to bring every concern to me in prayer and express gratitude for past blessings. My promise is inexplicable peace.

Let's trust Him together as we declare His faithfulness. Speak out my promises to counter any accusation of the enemy.

My Active Response
- Consider, where does my deliverance really come from?
- Read Psalm 121, 2 Corinthians 10.

My Worship
- "In the Presence of Jehovah" - Vicky Yohe
- "God, I Look to You" - New Wine Worship

Journal

Day
8

WALK WITH ME
AND BE ENCOURAGED

Why are you in despair, O my soul?
And why have you become disturbed within me?
Hope in God, for I shall yet praise Him,
the help of my countenance and my God. Psalm 42:11

Your heart is a strong force in your life, did you know that? It carries you into your future. I asked you to keep a close watch on the direction it is taking you.

When your heart is sad and discouraged, I am unable to work. You make me redundant because you are weak and crippled under the pressure of the problems rather than hopeful and expectant of the possibilities of my promises.

You alone can make that choice to win or lose, be sad or joyful. I have made everything available for you to win. Will you choose my way of walking through this?

The secret is in my Word. I have even gone ahead to choose for you. I chose life for you. This will not only benefit you but will set your children and their children after them up for eternal good. Your choice of courage today, to win, will set the stage of success for those coming after you.

Besides your family, other believers who are watching you scale the wall of opposition will ride on your example and choose to take a leap at winning as well. Even better, those who have not yet come to me will see how good I am to you, how my words always bear fruit, and they will be convinced that our Father is a good God, contrary to what the devil peddles.

Your world is rife with discouragement, but you must continue to choose the life I made available to you through my word.

When the devil dumps sickness on you, what will you choose? I bore the pain, so you will not have to. Thirty-nine lashes scourged my back. Spear gashes, wounded my side. Rusty nails punctured my flesh, bore holes in my hands and feet, all so that you will not have to. Thorny wreath tore at my brow dripping life in my blood. Will you receive that sacrifice of life and choose what I gave up for you to have?

When the father of lies plagues your mind with doubts of my provision, telling you the only way is "heaven helps those who help themselves," what will you choose? Will you remember I laid down my glory, came from streets paved with gold, pearly gates, and crystal streams, to walk along dusty and cobbled roads.

Presented with meagre meals, I fed multitudes, all to show you that I will look after you even when you have little. Will you expect good from me and revel in all I have done for you?

My Active Response
- What determines my joy? Circumstances or the Word?
- Read 1Samuel 30; Psalm 127

My Worship
- "10,000 Reasons" - Matt Redman
- "Ever Be" - Aaron Shust

Journal

<table>
<tr><td>Day
9</td><td># I AM YOUR CHAMPION</td></tr>
</table>

Many are saying of my soul, "There is no deliverance for him in God." (Selah). But You, O LORD, are a shield about me, my glory, and the One who lifts my head. I was crying to the LORD with my voice, and He answered me from His holy mountain. (Selah). I lay down and slept, I awoke, for the LORD sustains me.
Psalm 3:2-5

Do you ever wonder what goes on around you when you sleep? What can you do about your safety when you are deep in sleep? You woke up this morning, you did nothing to keep your breath from ceasing during the night. You didn't nudge yourself to wake up when the first light of dawn broke through the clouds. You did not make your lungs perform its appointed purpose of moving air through your body, or your heart, pumping blood through your body. I did all that for you.

I kept your vital organs working, made certain there was air supplied for your breathing and all these are things you take for granted.

If I looked out for you that way, will I ever abandon you? I station my sentinels as you sleep to guard you from harm. Will I not hear when you call?

Here I am, seated with you. I am in this battle, fighting on your behalf. Have I not told you to hold your peace and let me fight for you? My battle plans are revolutionary. I kill several birds with a stone because I work from a higher perspective. Your view is one dimensional. I rise high, higher than the eagle and can see the different facets of the issue.

My children leaving Egypt thought they were doomed, between the Red Sea and Pharaoh's army. You have a similar saying- "between the rock and a hard place." That portended doom, but I always have an exit strategy that surpasses your imagination.

Who knew I would part the waters; aqua cavalry saluting my wondrous Majesty? Paving a way for my brood. Dry solid ground at the bottom of the sea was my plan for them to walk on.

Pharaoh and his horse regiment trooped into my crosshairs. Once and for all, the cup of his arrogance and hatred towards my children filled up fast. It ran over, he overplayed his hand He overlooked one small, but gravely critical detail, the original message.

The Father's request was for Pharaoh to release His people so they would go and worship Him. He forgot all about the plagues, saw an inescapable trap, the Red Sea, charging with zeal to hem them in. That noose hanged him.

The chariots' wheels got stuck where the feet of God's family walked dry and firm. Such spectacular sight! Victory won. God promised the Egyptians would be no more!

In like manner, if would you trust me with these issues, I will bring you out rejoicing. There will be no doubt whose Hands delivered you. I will rescue you, and you will rest your feet on my promised trophy, the footstool of the enemy's head. Rest in me, I am watching over you.

My Active Response
- Meditate on God's gift of rest.
- Read Exodus 14; Psalm 3.

My Worship
- "Oceans" - Hillsong United
- "Whom Shall I Fear (God of Angel Armies)" - Chris Tomlin

Journal

KEEP YOUR FOCUS ON ME

*My spirit is broken, my days are extinguished, the grave
is ready for me. "Surely mockers are with me, and my eye gazes
on their provocation. "Lay down, now, a pledge for me with
Yourself; who is there that will be my guarantor?*
Job 17:1-3

Does it feel like you are done for if the situation does not change? Do you feel the cold snarky fingers of the enemy tighten on your neck, his noose slowly deflating the air in your lungs? It may feel like that, but you're here and I AM here.

The situation is not half as gloomy as the storm he wells up. He roars as a lion, but I AM the Lion of the Tribe of Judah. Nothing he tries will ever outwit my power in you. Only remember who and whose you are.

You are my treasured possession, the one etched on the palm of my hands. I set out the pathways of your life even before you were formed in your mother's womb. I knew you from the foundation of the earth and you are precious to me.

What will I not give for you? The Father sent me from out Himself to demonstrate His love for you. When I was returning to the Father, I left behind my Holy Spirit as the guarantee of our ever-constant presence and help.

It does not matter how hard things get, my word must continue to be your foundation and weapon through the battle. I fought and won the war already. Did I not go into hell to confront the prince of darkness? Freed the captives and took back what he stole from the first Adam?

I am called the second Adam; I restored the Father's plan for Eden. My death restored the goodness and bounty of Eden. Will you trust and reach out in faith to occupy and inherit the Garden once again? All the devil wants to do is drive you out of that Garden which our Father wisely and deliberately planted just for you.

Never lose sight of who you are and what is yours. I already paid for it. You will only short-change yourself if you allow the enemy to intimidate you out of your inheritance.

What will it be today? Fear or faith? Praise or pout? I want you to choose faith, it makes it all worth it! I am here. I will carry you when you become faint. I will strengthen you when you become weak. Together, let's take the land today.

Focus on the promises. Put them on continuous play in your heart and mouth. See yourself thriving because of these precious promises, which can never fail. Today is your day to overcome. Every day, IS your day to overcome. Plant your feet on the soil of these promises in the spirit and take possession of what is yours. I already said wherever the soles of your feet shall tread upon, I have given you as an inheritance. So, take back what is yours today. That is how the fight of faith is fought and won.

My Active Response
- Think about this, what is my faith worth?
- Read Isaiah 46.

My Worship
- "Diamonds" - Hawk Nelson
- "Remind Me Who I Am" - Jason Gray

I AM YOUR LIGHT

Peter said to Him, "Lord, if it is You, command me to come to You on the water." And He said, "Come!" And Peter got out of the boat and walked on the water and came toward Jesus. But seeing the wind, he became frightened, and beginning to sink, he cried out, "Lord, save me!" Immediately Jesus stretched out His hand and took hold of him, and said to him, "You of little faith, why did you doubt?" Matthew 14:28-31

Beloved, what are you focused on? Me, my words, or the troubles? No trouble has power over you except what you give it. No trial can destroy you except one you surrender your will to. The power is in my word. Will you believe me?

I knew the trials would come. I knew the winds would rage and the waves swell, but like the good Shepherd I am,

I am right here with you. When you pay too much attention to the challenges, you magnify them. I know.

In the Garden of surrender, Gethsemane, the troubles threatened to overwhelm me, but I refocused on what was important, the word of the Father. The One who said, "who will go for these people?" To which I responded, "here I am, send me." How could I forget His command or lose sight of the bigger picture? Eternity depended on me.

Even when it felt like the darkness had won; the freezing breeze of loneliness arrested my heart at the thought of Him deserting me on the cross; all for the sake of my siblings, you are one of them. The unwavering guarantee of His word kept my head in the plan. Only three nights and three days, and we dispossess the evil plotter of his scheme and win forever!

Do you believe in the power of my words, "IT IS FINISHED!?" Nothing else to be done. Just like the Father, I am resting in the position He gave me, and my Name that He exalted above all others will always bring Satan and his evil devises to their knees. You only need to accept and believe what I already accomplished for you.

Simply call out my Name when the trial seems fierce. Look to my word which is the vessel holding my power available for you. That was how I won. Holding on to every word of the Father. Doing everything I hear Him say do. Believing that He can never lie. Trusting that His love will make a way.

Ever true to His word. On the final day in that cold, but appointed and esteemed tomb, His Spirit came for me. His Ruach, breath, did what He did when He formed Adam. He breathed life into me, and my life form took on new life. I was born again of His Spirit, keys in hand. I beat down the

Tempter on his turf. Forever, I destroyed all his works and power over you!

What trouble can dare take you down? Look to me, I establish and complete your faith by my words.

My Active Response
- Do I truly believe that God's word suffices in my troubles?
- Read Isaiah 43; Hebrews 12:1-3.

My Worship
- "Just Be Held" - Casting Crowns
- "Praise You in This Storm" - Casting Crowns

Journal

BE PATIENT
IN THE WAIT

Whom have I in heaven but You? And besides You, I desire
nothing on earth. My flesh and my heart may fail, but God is the
strength of my heart and my portion forever. Psalm 73:25,26

How unfair, you think, is it when those who live corrupt
lives always seem to be the ones getting ahead in the world.
That is what it is, mere appearance. But you never mind
that.

Like anything the devil offers, it always comes at a cost.
Eternity, ultimately, if they refuse me as Lord. The devil is
the father of lies and knows no other way to hold people
under his control than to make them believe he alone can
offer them what I already made theirs. Ironic, right?

Let's focus on you. My promises to you will surely come to pass. Remember Abraham, my friend? He came out with me on a limb. I was not like any god he had ever known. He had no inkling where I was taking him, yet he trusted me and came out with me.

I promised and showed him his generations as the stars in the sky, descendants like the sand on the seashore. Not knowing how all these will happen, he believed, even to the point that I would raise Isaac from the dead.

Though he fumbled some in the wait, yielded to pressure, he re-established himself in the promise and I brought my promise to pass. I reordered his thinking by naming him a new name so he could focus on the prize.

He did all he knew to do to hold on in faith. Yet, it took time for my promise to come to pass. Many things are involved in the performance of my word and every promise has its timing. Be patient and wait for it. Keep my word before your eyes and hide it in your heart. Let your mouth not speak anything contrary. Ishmael was the result of impatience. That was not my perfect will.

Look through my word. How my people suffered because they would not be patient? Remember the Golden Calf in the wilderness? They bowed the knee to the god of their materialism, they thought I was late, perhaps I had abandoned them. Yet I was building a hedge for them, a protection against the charms of the enemy. A system for my relationship with them and for theirs, one to another.

Anything apart from my word and my will is temporal. I have shown you the way to success-continually looking upon my word, thinking upon my word, and professing my word. Don't be frustrated about or envious of the apparent success of evildoers. Take my word for it, it never lasts!

Make the necessary adjustments and position yourself; your heart, mouth, and mind, where my words are the authority in every situation you find yourself in.

My Active Response
- Am I envious of the success of others? What will this cost me?
- Read Psalms 73; Genesis 16

My Worship
- "Good, Good Father" - Chris Tomlin
- "Worthy of It All" - Kalley Heiligenthal

Journal

I HAVE OVERCOME
THE WORLD FOR YOU

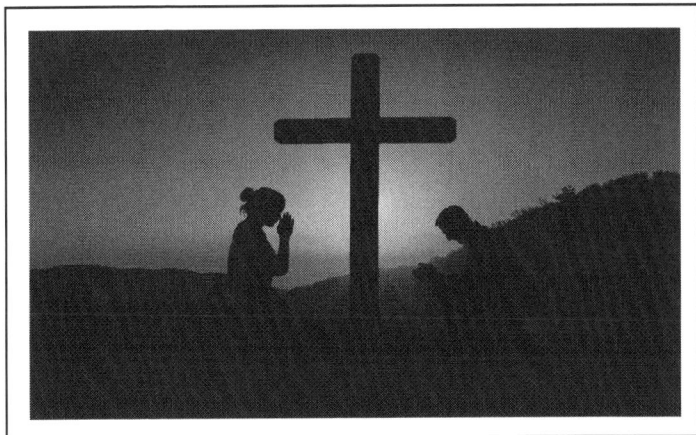

The LORD is the one who goes ahead of you;
He will be with you. He will not fail you or forsake you.
Do not fear or be dismayed." Deuteronomy 31:8

Dear child, have you considered how frequently I require of
you to put fear out of your life? I say so, because I am aware
of the reality of fear and its power to defraud you of your
destiny. Fear pulls a veil between you and the Father's
comforting presence. You must however choose the power
of the Greater One resident in you over an illusion. I call it
so because it is not real!

The truth of my Word is that I overcame for you. I
encouraged you to be cheerful despite these challenges.
Satan will not stop. Let that sink into you right now. He will

keep on devising means to wear you out. Remember what I said to Peter. How I let him in on the secret plans of the enemy. Satan made a demand to agitate all of you who are called by my name to the point that you will give up. He wants to place all the pressure he can muster on you to frustrate you out of your inheritance. The reality is, he is enraged with envy over your destiny.

I already made available all you need to be successful in life. But this you must know; you will have to fight for some things. Just as the thick unyielding wall wrapped around Jericho, the enemy will raise up walls of opposition around some of my promises and plans for you. This is where you must make a choice. Faith in my word or fear of what the devil might do to you. Notice I said might, because he makes it so convincing that he can hurt you. If you keep my word strong on your heart and ready in your mouth, you will extinguish those lies and threats.

I have the keys of death and hell. As my child, I have given the same right to you. Always remember, there is nothing to be afraid of. I have gone before you to seize back the authority he extorted from Adam. I have recovered it and made it available to you. Do you believe me or are the snarls of a defeated copycat noisier than my conquering roar?

I am your Saviour. I have paid the price already. Emmanuel is my name; I am always with you. He has no power over you. Do you ever remember that he has been placed underneath your feet? Why then do you give him so much credit? The fraud that he is, he has sold a lie, and many have bought into it and are living like he is the triumphant one.

Rise up and be who I paid for you to be. You are the home of the Creator of the universe. Who can withstand

Him? The One in you is greater than Satan and his band of demons. Rejoice in that truth and stand firm. Praise him out of town! He can't stand your praise. Let the symbol of my victory, the cross, always be before you to remind you of the exalted position the Father gave you in my Name. You are above the wickedness of this world. Satan's neck is beneath your feet! That should make you do a twirl today.

My Active Response
- Who are you? Ponder your identity in Christ
- Read Luke 22:31-34

My Worship
- "How Many Kings" - Downhere
- "You Laid Aside Your Majesty" - Hillsong

PRAISE YOUR WAY THROUGH

Sing praise to the LORD, you His godly ones, and give thanks to His holy name. For His anger is but for a moment, His favor is for a lifetime; Weeping may last for the night, but a shout of joy comes in the morning.
Psalm 30:4,5

My dear one, do you remember where it says praise looks good on you? When you praise, you bring me on the scene. Praise demonstrates your faith in me and my ability to create a passageway for you through the issues.

Don't buy the lie that our Father is angry with you. He is not. He sent me to die for you. What other expression of love could there be? He did it to completely lay to rest the cycle of rebellion that made Him punish the ancients. They were called out of Egypt and constantly provoked Him to anger by their rejection of His rule over them. For four hundred years, He kept silent. He gave them over to their inordinate desires. They wanted other rulers besides Him, still He protected them and provided for them.

Your story is different. You are not under the law. You are under the grace I made available for you. It does not matter what you do or do not do, my grace was freely given. All I ask is for you to believe and receive it by faith.

Let it be your assurance that the Father and I love you and we will always be there for you and provide for you. It may appear tough right now, but rest assured, it is all working out for good.

Just as a seed does not become a full tree the day it was planted, so the promises I give you must be allowed to run their full course. Life has an order, and you must allow the order to bring you its full benefits. Every seed carries the end inside it. My promises hold the expected end you desire.

When the process seems long, praise me. The seed, when it is planted, cannot complain of the darkness and delay while in the ground. It understands that is the natural order of its life. So, do not gripe when it appears like the promises are taking time. Dream of the end. Prepare for the performance of the promise. Let nothing deter you. I will be magnified in your praise, and I will attend to your prayers. Your attitude will make or break you. You have a choice to make. Praise or pout?

I have given you the way out. I asked you to choose life. Everyday life presents you with difficulties. How you process them will reflect what you choose. If you lift me up higher than these issues, you have chosen life. You affirm that no trial can destroy you. If you see an impossible situation, you cannot get out of, you have chosen death and you tie my hands. My angels only respond to words of life. So, speak life in praise, and praise your way into your breakthrough. Praise regardless of what you're feeling.

My Active Response
- What will keep my praise on even when the situation looks grim?
- Read Psalm 33

My Worship
- "This is Amazing Grace" - Phil Wickham
- "Lord I Run to You" - Alvin Slaughter

Journal

SAFE BENEATH
MY WINGS

In You, O LORD, I have taken refuge;
Let me never be ashamed; In Your righteousness deliver me.
Incline Your ear to me, rescue me quickly; Be to me a rock of
strength, a stronghold to save me. Psalm 31:1,2

Today, child, I want to thank you for trusting and crying out to me. I am here. I have never left your side. I assured you of my constant presence. I felt every pain and noticed every tear. I heard every sigh. My eyebrow, never raised to the questions in your heart. You called because you knew I was your only way out of this. I alone can carry you through this.

My wisdom, which laid the foundations of the earth and keep them running still is available to direct you. I asked you to come boldly to me. My grace is available for you to lead you over triumphantly. Take nothing for granted, I can show you the way step-by-step. I am satisfied by your success. Seeing you joyful brings me joy. My strength is made strong in your weakness. When you depend on me to save you, you affirm your faith in who I am.

Your shame is not an option because you bear my Name. You are my very own. Your shame will be my shame. It will mirror me as unreliable, fickle, a sham. Have I not said that when your heart burrows and nestles into my word, it is like constructing a house on a deep secure boulder?

The rolling and heaving torrents of adversity cannot demolish it. You always have a part in our alliance. You must keep my word in your heart so I can remain that anchor which keeps you steady despite what you're seeing and the issues that boggle your mind.

My word gives you courage in the storm. My word keeps you strong and bold in the process. When I hear you return my word to me in prayer, you get my attention! I bend over and press my ear to your mouth. You invite me into intimacy with you. This is when I can reveal the exit strategy to you. This is how I cover you with that peace that makes no natural sense.

That peace is my kâbôd. My shield. My bow. It will protect and promote you through the trial. It will hide you from the torment of the enemy. He will not see you because you are beneath the shadow of my wings. To get to you, he will need to take me out; and that is an impossible thought to even conceive!

Know you are safe. Rest in me my child, I am always here. Remember David's strategy. He set me always before him. He knew I would never abdicate my position at his right hand. His conclusion? He couldn't be shaken.

Remember what I told Habakkuk? Set me before you as well by placing my words where you can easily see them, your eyes being the gateway to your heart. What are you focussed on?

My Active Response
- How fastened to His words is my heart?
- Read Psalm 91

My Worship
- "How Deep the Father's Love for Us" -Nicole Nordeman
- "I Will Run to You" - Alvin Slaughter

Journal

MY CROSS REDEEMED YOU

Do not let your heart be troubled; believe in God, believe also in Me. John 14:1

It's another new day. One filled with the potential for all good things and an abundant measure of my blessing. One for which my grace is poured out for you to bear and triumph through whatever you are carrying. Did you read or understand my word in John 14:1 as a command? Or did you understand it as a suggestion?

Have you pondered the price of the cross? The shame and the scorn? The spitting and the lashing? The crown of thorns digging into my brow, my side gashed to pour out the witnesses of my love for you, water, and blood?

Accept my love for you as a surety for your trust in me. No holds barred. I poured out my all. I gave it all up. Most heart wrenching, my lifeline, fellowship with my Father!

I paid for your peace with thirty-nine stripes. Enduring agonising pain, betrayal from one chosen and loved, I redeemed you for the thirty pieces of silver he accepted to turn me over to the enemy.

My heart broke to mend yours. Not just mine, our Father's too. He had to look away because His eyes are too pure to look on sin. The pain of our separation broke His heart, all because He had to establish your heart in His love. The love, which made Him pay the price to buy back your legacy from the father of lies.

Know this, Satan has absolutely nothing on you. Everything he could hold up in accusation against you have been countered. He will try. Try to make you feel unworthy. The good news is, it is not dependent on you; what you did or didn't do It is about my love for you. My love and sacrifice have made you worth everything.

Whenever he comes to taunt you, remind him of how I knocked out his teeth, broke his back and seized from him the keys of death and hell. To rub his face in it, I gave you those keys. Don't hand them back by believing his lies. That is all he has.

Think daily on the price I paid. It cost me my life, but you are worth every jot of blood. You are worth every degree of pain.

Focus on the benefits that came to you. With His fingers, the Father ripped the curtain of separation in two and invited you to come boldly to Him. He is neither angry with nor irritated by you. The cross is the ultimate dimension of His love for you.

Believe in Him, believe in me. Let your heart roost in the reality of our love. We will die for you a lifetime over; we love you that much. You are worth the sacrifice!

My Active Response
- How can I rest more in His immeasurable love for me?
- Read Psalm 103; Hebrews 4:14-16

My Worship
- "Open Heavens" - Gateway
- "He Alone Is Worthy" - Alvin Slaughter

Journal

MY TRUTH PIERCES
EVERY DARKNESS

I have given them Your word; and the world has hated them,
because they are not of the world, even as I am not of the world. I
do not ask You to take them out of the world, but to keep them
from the evil one. They are not of the world, even as I am not of
the world. Sanctify them in the truth; Your word is truth. John
17:14-17

Good morning my lovely one. Is it a good morning? How
do you receive the gift of a new day? Through the eyes of
your pain, or the truth of our Father's promises? His word
is always true. Your 'opposer', the devil, lives only to cast a
doubt in your heart about the truth.

Your steps will be hindered when you try to process the truth through the lens of a lie. Truth is light, lies hide in the shadows of darkness. You miscalculate your way when you are trying to walk in the darkness. You stub your toes and pain is unavoidable. The truth of our Father's word will have no chance when you try to believe it through a lie. Darkness appears tangible, heavy, and thick. It looms large, but the first glimmer of the light of dawn, or the stream of light at the flick of a switch squelches its intimidation.

The devil's lies appear intimidating and more tangible than the Father's truth. But that's all it is, a mirage. Don't let him pressure you into laying down what's real, the truth of our Father's word.

Paul wrote to the church in Corinth about this. The devil and people can oppose the truth all they want, but no one can do anything against the truth. It remains what it is, the truth!

There is a theory in the world stating the three stages of truth. First it is ridiculed, then violently opposed, and finally accepted as being self-evident. I was mocked and spat at for saying the temple, my body, will be destroyed, but after three days, will be rebuilt.

My nail pierced hands and feet, my scarred side are proof that my word is true. Their violent opposition proved it true. Of their own will, they crucified me. The lie Satan spread opposed him and affirmed my truth. Those who saw me rise back to life attested to my identity.

The devil played right into the Father's hand. "Had he known," the scribes recorded, "he would not have crucified the Lord of glory." Little did he know that he was fulfilling the truth. At the cross, the centurion affirmed the truth when he saw the evidence.

That only which our Father could do. Dead raised to life, curtain rend in two by His hand reaching down from heaven, darkness covering the earth. A full display of His salvation, and grief at the price He was willing to pay for them, for you!

Though they still tried to deny the truth, they couldn't deny seeing what He had done. When I arose by the power of His Spirit, they lied still. Paid to silence the soldiers and accused my brothers of stealing my body from the tomb. But you are the result of the performance of that truth. You are here. Live the victory I already won for you. Let my truth outshine the darkness of Satan's lies. Live in my light.

My Active Response
- What is truth in my situation today?
- Read through the narrative of the Passion of Jesus in all the books of the Gospel.

My Worship
- "Amazed" - Lincoln Brewster
- "It Is Well" - Kristene DiMarco & Bethel Music

TRUST AND
DEPEND ON ME

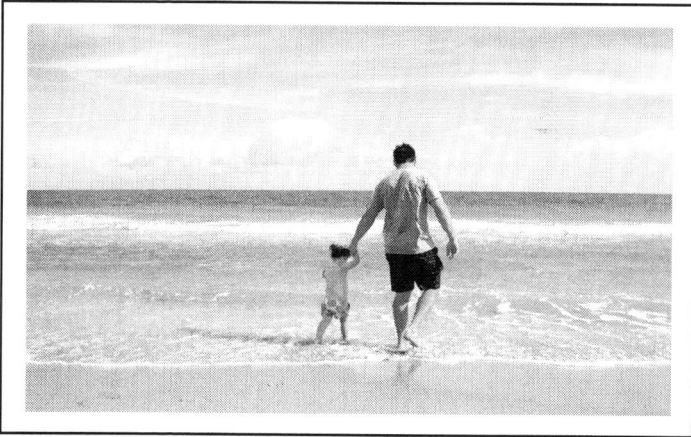

*For God so loved the world, that He gave His only begotten
Son, that whoever believes in Him shall not perish, but have
eternal life. John 3:16*

Beloved, how much do you believe I love you? Remember
as a child Mama asking the same question, stretching out
her arms, showing you the expanse of her love for you?
Same is my love and our Father's for you. I stretched out my
arms wide and took those rusty nails cutting through and
bursting open my veins because of the extent of my love for
you. The distance between the East and the West.

Do you understand what it means to give your ultimate?
Have you ever given up what meant the most to you in all

your life? When our Father asked Abraham to sacrifice Isaac, it was not news to him. All the gods of his people would require that anyway. But how would our God show He was different? He had to provide. He had to give. He had to rescue what meant the world to Abraham.

Abraham proved his faith. He had been walking with our Father. He recognized He was different from all the other gods. He knew he could count on God. He set his heart on a miracle. He was sure of a resurrection. He hoped against hope that our Father would stay true to His promises. Abraham was given his name because of his destiny, the father of nations. Ishmael was not the chosen seed. You see, our Father does things well. He is not irrational. You can grasp the purpose of His ways and thoughts, which are much higher than yours!

He assured you He will forever only think good thoughts towards you. He will forever only lead you to a good end. He will never harm you; He will never hurt you. When He appears silent, trust Him still. He is working in you a good work. He is refining you for His glory. He is calling you higher.

Sin is a heavy weight under which this whole world is crumpling. Whether they know it or not, they are looking for salvation. They want out of the senselessness and hopelessness. They crave answers. Your trials equip you with grace and compassion. You have tasted our God and you know He is good.

You can bear witness to His character. He drew you out of the depth of despair. He gives you hope. His love is always on you. His affection is always toward you. It does not matter how tough the challenge feels, always remember this truth, His love for you extends to eternity. His heart bled at the expense of His love, but His power is greater than death. His mercy made a way. His counsel outwitted the adversary. He has been carrying you before you were ever planted in your mother's belly. Will He not already have a way out for you? This is grace.

My Active Response

- What is grace?
- Read Genesis 22:1-19.

My Worship

- "Heart Like Heaven" - Hillsong United
- "Jesus" - Chris Tomlin

Journal

DO NOT BE DECEIVED

*The LORD will deliver them up before you, and you shall do
to them according to all the commandments which I have
commanded you. Be strong and courageous, do not be afraid or
tremble at them, for the LORD your God is the one who goes with
you. He will not fail you or forsake you."*
Deuteronomy 31:5,6

It's another day of great expectation! Another day to receive
grace for the road you're on. When I was leaving this earth,
I prayed to the Father for each one of you. I asked Him to
keep you from the evil one. Not take you out of this world,
because you are the hope of this world, believe it! I

promised you my Spirit. Our Father's dynamo. His power at work in you.

On a mission, He tore through the stone rolled to the mouth of the tomb, not even that could stop Him! He pulled back the burial shroud; He the Spirit of life and grace, puffed His RUACH, Himself, into that grave. Death lost its grip. The last straw broken. Satan's shame complete. He lost. I arose triumphant. I had completed the assignment. The price was paid, and Satan no longer has power over you.

Will he stop trying to make you feel like you lost? Go figure. He goes about as a roaring lion, remember. Always looking for someone who doesn't know the truth about their inheritance through me. He has nothing on you. The same Spirit who completed the work of redemption, He who raised me from the grave and restored life to me, He is the same Spirit the Father sent to be in you and with you. That same power that raised me from the grave, the same power He displayed at creation is in you.

Who do you think you are? A defeated, helpless nobody? You are the child of God. His image and likeness. One with His ability and mind. All of Him is inside you. That is no defeated nobody! You are a victor, a winner.

In ignorance, you might have bought into a lie, but see now what you can do to the enemy who dared to afflict you. See the hell you can send him send him and his minions to.

Think, think, think on whose power is available to you. Meditate – think, say and act – on who is in you and let the real Lion roar. A lion's cub has the seed of the mother and father in it. It is as much king as its father. It learns to take down the prey without fear. Its instincts tell it how to attack, and the prey is no match for it. So are you. Satan is no match for you; the Greater One inside you sees to that. He is with you and cannot abandon you. You are His treasury.

He poured His life into you. He gave you His authority and mandate to look after His creation. See to it that His world retains the order He set in place at creation.

Never doubt who you are and what you have in our Father. Satan wants you to believe otherwise. Don't get caught in the lies.

My Active Response
- Look in the mirror today and tell the person looking back at you who they are.
- Meditate on 1John 4:4.

My Worship
- "Steady My Heart" - Kari Jobe
- "I Am Not Alone" - Kari Jobe

BE ENCOURAGED
IN ME

*And the great dragon was thrown down, the serpent of old
who is called the devil and Satan, who deceives the whole world;
he was thrown down to the earth, and his angels were thrown
down with him. Then I heard a loud voice in heaven, saying,
"Now the salvation, and the power, and the kingdom of our God
and the authority of His Christ have come, for the accuser of our
brethren has been thrown down, he who accuses them before our
God day and night. And they overcame him because of the blood
of the Lamb and because of the word of their testimony, and
they did not love their life even when faced with death.*
Revelation12:9-11

What are you saying about yourself? Believe it or not, today is a day of victory! Every day is. Look who's bound for eternal damnation. The old scoundrel, Satan. He is a deceiver and a cheat. He swore an oath to see you fall. He has committed his life to see you banished from our Father in eternity.

He lies in wait in the shadows to pounce on you with lies and accusations. He digs up dirt on you and makes you feel shame. He hands you a hammer to drive down the nail of lie in the pretend coffin he thinks he has you.

Don't fall for it! It's all make-believe. He flashes before you blunders of the past that are already under the Blood. Sins that have been drowned in the sea of forgetfulness. He revives the regret; hurls you back in the pit of pity. Don't help him by burrowing yourself in his slime of shame. He's the one who has been cast down. His future is in the searing lake of sulphur.

I already asked you not to be discouraged, you are an O-V-E-R-C-O-M-E-R! My word in your mouth is your victory. My blood is your victory. My perfect sacrifice paid the price so Satan cannot have anything on you.

I said you will not see shame and you will stand your ground against him. I remain your Advocate, your Safeguard and Shield against him.

His MO is to play mind games. He stabs at your integrity and drags you to his level. Never forget it, his best view are the soles of your feet, don't fret or carry the guilt over his accusations.

He is the only one keeping that account, and you, if you get into it with him. Dress up; cover yourself. Take the Father's armour and stand your ground. He is nothing more than a gnat to squish underfoot when you are well dressed.

Sit back in your place right here next to me. You are part of a higher League.

Trap his foul propositions in your head. Yes, those ones that tag you 'undeserving', 'not enough'. Peel the labels off you. It was never about you.

He thinks he can wound the Father through you. Our Father's choice of you when He called you was more than about you.

We were created for His praise and glory. With you well dressed, I ask you to think on, things that are true, pure, lovely just, honest, of good report, virtuous and praiseworthy.

Don't stay silent. Wield your weapons, your sword through my Spirit, to flick of wrong labels he wants to stick on you. Raise up your shield of faith and snuff out the flames of lies and accusations, he fires at you.

You are equipped for the attack.

My Active Response
- Read Ephesians 6:10-18.
- Memorize Philippians 4:6-9

My Worship
- "Rise" - Danny Gokey
- "Remind Me Who I Am" - Jason Gray

Journal

YOUR FELLOWSHIP
WITH ONE ANOTHER

I thank my God always, making mention of you in my prayers, because I hear of your love and of the faith which you have toward the Lord Jesus and toward all the saints; and I pray that the fellowship of your faith may become effective through the knowledge of every good thing which is in you for Christ's sake. Philemon1:4-6

Who is your companion? Yourself? Get your head out of the ditch. Don't hide the treasure inside you away from the world. You are my vessel of honour, filled with my goodness to pour out to others for their elevation. I have deposited too much in you to hide away.

The father of lies wants to isolate you so he can wear you down. Your faith and love are meant to be shared.

Iron sharpens iron, as one friend sharpens the other. Two metals rubbing against each other become sharpened. But you become depressed and even more discouraged when you are isolated. Let another lift you up. Sure, I am the Friend made for tough times, and I am always here, but I also asked you not to forsake getting together with others in the faith, and to also encourage one another.

Just as you were made to help others rise from the blues, so were they made to help you see the brighter side of life.

You are to be intentional about participating in the life of another, whether they are Christians or not. Be a 'lifter-upper'. Be a positive influence, to help them remember the sun is always shinning no matter how dark and thick the clouds may look.

The Father, the Spirit and I have shown you by our example, we are always in harmony with one another. So must you be with others whose faith are in me, whose eyes are on me. They will help you see the truth about yourself, they will reconnect you to the good inside you. They will remind you of who and whose you are. They will reach down and help you climb back up from the pits.

Your faith grows when in fellowship with other Christians. That word fellowship means pouring out to others as they pour out to you.

David in the Psalms wrote about the anointing that flows in the assembly of believers who have a common goal and desire. Our Father releases endless life, which is only found in community with others, that is how He made humans. He said it was not good that Adam was alone, and He made Eve. As well, you become better in the company of others like yourself. Then your faith becomes more powerful, and you are renewed and recharged.

Be a friend to gain a friend. Pour out and receive. Don't be a stagnant pool, let the life-giving stream in you flow out and receive the stream of life from others

My Active Response
- Read Psalm 133.
- Seek out someone who needs encouragement and lift them up with something meaningful.

My Worship
- "Tell Your Heart To Beat Again" - Danny Gokey
- "Give Me Faith" - Elevation Worship

Journal

Day	YOUR FRAGRANT
22	OFFERING OF
	THANKSGIVING

> *Then Jonah prayed to the LORD his God from the stomach of*
> *the fish, and he said, "I called out of my distress to the LORD,*
> *and He answered me. I cried for help from the depth of Sheol;*
> *You heard my voice .... But I will sacrifice to You. With the*
> *voice of thanksgiving. That which I have vowed I will pay.*
> *Salvation is from the LORD."*
> *Jonah 2:1,2, 9*

Good morning my dear one. When you woke up this
morning, what were the first thoughts on your heart?
Despair or thanksgiving? If despair, your heart is focused

on the storms around you. Thanksgiving, your heart is in the right place. Your focus is on me, as it should be.

Asaph, one of David's worship leaders, and my prophet, points you in the right direction in the Psalms. He talks about "offering to God a sacrifice of thanksgiving."

A sacrifice was a pleasurable offering to our Father. It connected the offeror to Him. Asaph points to a sacrifice different from the usual sin offering of animals. He talks about thanksgiving. A most appealing gesture to the Father!

Thanksgiving takes your heart from a place of lack and want to that of appreciation of all that our Father has done for you. It refocuses you from lack to provision. Thanksgiving centers your heart on the Father and His ability to save and provide salvation in every situation. It raises your hand to the One who alone can save and deliver.

Remember when I suggested we fed the multitude who had been with me in the countryside because they had been with us awhile. My brothers only saw shortage, I saw an opportunity for our Father to be glorified. My connection with Him was thanksgiving. I offered the little available to Him who had the power to multiply. I gave thanks. He did not fail. My faith in Him to perform His word and provide was rewarded. He released the miracle right in the hands of my brothers. As they gave out, the dinner multiplied.

The lad, generous to pour out his supply, was the most blessed that day. His act of giving set in motion my sacrifice of thanksgiving. His heart believed, having heard me teach about the Kingdom of our God. He came forward with his meal because he believed his little could do much. He understood that with God, all things were possible. He supernaturally understood the grace of multiplication. He gave willingly. He extended his hand out and up. He offered the sacrifice first.

Thanksgiving involves extending your hand to the One who has all power to dispense favour towards you. It acknowledges the love and ability of our Father. It worships His greatness. It reduces the problem to nothing and increases His provision to everything. It's about your heart. Set it on the right thing. Give thanks to our Father. It is sweet perfume to Him.

My Active Response
- Read Psalm 50.
- Spend time in thanksgiving. Recount by writing out God's goodness towards me.

My Worship
- "Give Thanks" - Don Moen
- "You Raise Me Up" - Selah

Journal

Day	THE MAJESTY OF
23	YOUR WORSHIP

Ascribe to the LORD, O families of the peoples,
Ascribe to the LORD glory and strength.
Ascribe to the LORD the glory of His name; Bring an offering
and come into His courts. Psalm 96:7,8

Have you ever really considered why the Father sacrificed me for you? Apart from what is written in the Holy Scripture, have you, for your own sake, considered what my death was meant to accomplish? Apart from your salvation that is.

It was about recovery. The recovery of generations that were stolen by the devil's deceit. Yes, so our Abba may recover sons and daughters for the Kingdom.

The same speaks for you. In your trials, rather than seeking our Father for the solutions He can give, why not offer Him what you can give, what He deserves.

When you give Him the worth due His Name and fame, He is extolled as the Highest of all, the Most High King,

The Psalmist invites you to "ascribe." Let's pause there for a bit. Ascribe involves a repositioning. It involves offering something to and placing upon the person you are ascribing a value or virtue to.

You have been invited to offer to God, our Father and Creator of the Universe, glory, and strength; the glory of His Name. Do you understand that? It is no lowly feat!

He gave me His Name. The Name above all names. At the mention of His Name, my Name, every knee must bow, every tongue must confess me as Lord. Miracles happen when you ascribe glory and strength to our God. You change, your situation changes. You receive strength for victory.

How do you do this? By taking an offering into His courts. Your arms stretched towards Him in respectful devotion. Your mouth confessing His majesty. Your situation bowing to His Lordship and yielding to His command.

The Psalmist tells you how to come into His courts; with praise. Coming into His courts sees you being ushered into His presence. Your thanksgiving takes you into His presence and you behold His glory. In His presence, all fear dispels, troubles fade away. The divine transaction happens. You lay down your burdens and He trades them for His glory. His glory cannot be hidden!

I asked you to give, so that a greater measure of your gift will become your benefit. A greater measure of strength will be added to you. Having seen Him face to face and received His glory, shame will be peeled off you. You will receive power to encounter the impossible. It is the greatest gift you can offer our Father. The gift of your love from a pure and devoted heart. That is why I said, "It is more blessed to give than to receive."

My Active Response
- Read Psalm 100.
- Spend extended time in worship today.

My Worship
- "Here in Your Presence" - Hosanna Music
- "As We Worship" - Bob Fitts

Journal

DRAW VICTORY FROM YOUR HEART

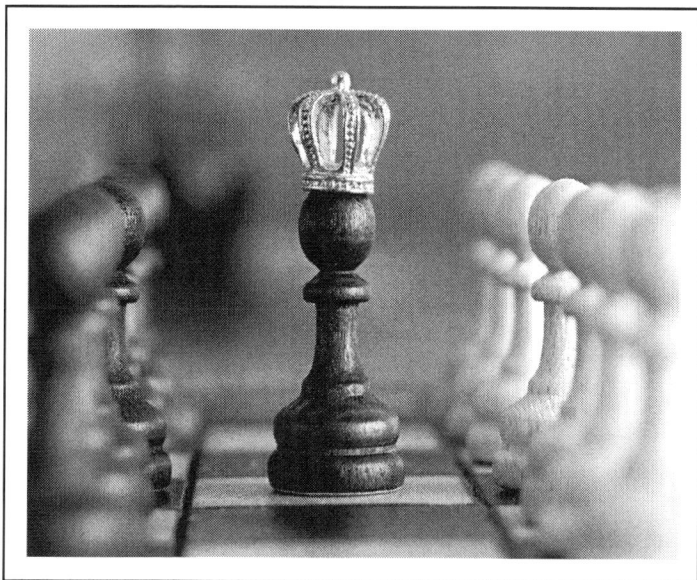

Through Him then, let us continually offer up a sacrifice of praise to God, that is, the fruit of lips that give thanks to His name. And do not neglect doing good and sharing, for with such sacrifices God is pleased. Hebrews 13:15,16

Victory begins in your heart. There is the seat of your faith, where my Spirit dwells. You are not mere flesh and blood. You are spirit and must fight your battles with spiritual artilleries. The dynamo of our Father is inside you. Always remember, that's who you are!

A feeble mind forfeits the win. No triumph, no conquest. If you feel pint-size in your mind, you will never dare take on a giant. You must set a patrol over your heart and watch that no malicious thoughts infiltrate and render you powerless.

With the Holy Spirit in you, offer God a sacrifice of praise. A sacrifice is often thought of as something you do when it is not convenient. Sure enough, praise is the last thing you want to do when faced with a challenge or when the enemy is bearing down hard on you.

A sacrifice was also what the Father required for appeasement before I offered the eternal one on your behalf. The Father is not angry with or offended by you. In fact, He is pleased with you and sees you pure and blameless because of the lens through which He looks at you. He gave you His Spirit. He no longer requires any sacrifice to ease any anger.

Turning inwards and drawing on the strength within positions you for a breakthrough. Standing with others who are walking through the same valley becomes seed for you and a harvest is bound to come.

The scriptures record how David's mighty men threatened to stone him after the Amalekites raided their camp and took their families captive. They had only recently been fighting together and had all wept together over their losses only to turn on him suddenly. Alone, abandoned, David reached inwards. The same power that energized him to slay Goliath spurred him to encourage himself. The word for victory came as a result. He walloped the Amalekites to their humiliation and recovered all who were abducted with every bit of property they made away with.

Same as Jehoshaphat, his battle strategy was praise in the face of the enemy. Hearing them, the enemy must have thought them silly. Little did they know what had just befallen them. God sent His power artillery, his fierce flaming force, who manipulated the minds of the enemy to the point where they were seeing double. Their comrades appeared like the enemy and they killed one another.

The fiercest battle changes course and no enemy can stand the wrath of our God. When His praise is sung, He arises in His might and fights for you whilst you look on.

Who can oppose Him?!

Praise is your greatest weapon because it confuses the enemy. The Father said that "surely they will gather," but because their gathering is not of Him, they are bound to be crushed for your sake. Gear your heart to praise your way through.

My Active Response
- Read 2 Chronicles 20.
- Spend time in worship today.

My Worship
- "Army of God" - Integrity Music
- "Mighty God" - Hosanna Music

Day 25 | JOY, YOUR COMPANION THROUGH THE JOURNEY

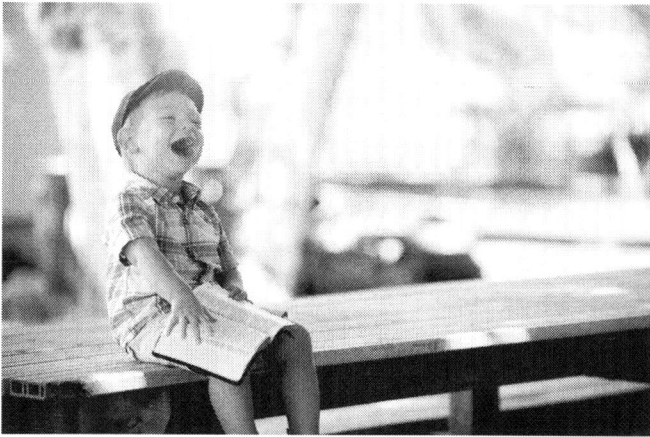

Rejoice always; pray without ceasing; in everything give thanks; for this is God's will for you in Christ Jesus. Do not quench the Spirit. 1 Thessalonians 5:16-19

Hear me child, nothing you are walking through is never-ending. Every adverse situation is subject to change, and there is no dead situation.

Every journey has an end. How you navigate the journey determines how you arrive. Refreshed or washed out. Regardless of the length of a journey, moaning through it, not seeing anything good about it, will only exasperate you. Your mind niggled with cares, instead of taking in the view and seizing occurring learning opportunities.

Maintaining your joy through the journey is what pleases the Father. In the scriptures, it is recorded that you rejoice no matter what. In every circumstance give thanks, it is the Father's will. It pleases Him because you affirm His might to deliver you through the situation.

However, when you moan and gripe, you smother the Holy Spirit within you and stifle His ability to help you.

You wonder, "how can I rejoice or even give thanks through this?" If all you magnify is what doesn't look or feel right with you today, then you only empower the enemy to deal you hard blows even more. You give him more incentive to knock you around.

Do you remember the scriptures saying God causes every detail of our lives to be continually woven together for good because we are His lovers called to fulfil His designed purpose? Each one of us has a role to play in the grand story the Father has written; the tapestry He has woven. He wastes nothing, not even your pain. He goes to work in you to polish you till He sees His image, me, in you.

If you submit those pangs on your heart to the Holy Spirit, through Him, our Father will develop fervent resilience in you, which develops a tenacious personality that keeps you watchful for God's next move. This sort of expectancy never fails to deliver. The guarantee of God's word lives in you and keeps an overflow of His love bubbling up with anticipation within you.

So, you must keep rejoicing to connect with your victory. Your thanksgiving makes you alert to the Holy Spirit inside you. He points out to you spot-on prayer strategies for the battle.

Your joyful thanksgiving keeps your mind on the truth that you are just reaching for the victory which has already been won for you. I asked you to rejoice because I overcame for you. I know it will not be easy, but like everything in the Father's Kingdom, you do it by faith. Press in and it will not just change your outlook, but also the atmosphere around you. So, just do it today. Laugh out loud at Satan and watch how you change.

My Active Response
- Read James 1:2-8; Ephesians 2:4-10 (Amplified Version)
- Spend time in worship today.

My Worship
- "Even When It Hurts" - Hillsong United
- "I Stand In Awe" - Bob Fitts

Journal

Day 26	HUMBLE YOURSELF THROUGH FASTING

My God, my God, why have You forsaken me? Far from my deliverance are the words of my groaning. O my God, I cry by day, but You do not answer; And by night, but I have no rest. Yet You are holy, O You who are enthroned upon the praises of Israel. In You our fathers trusted; They trusted and You delivered them. To You they cried out and were delivered; In You they trusted and were not disappointed. Psalm 22:1-5

Good morning, dear child. Have you ever wondered why praise is the Father's delight? He is surrounded by praise.

The creatures around His throne offer Him unending praise and worship. A flood of unspeakable joy flows in His presence. Pleasures abound at His right hand. If there was ever a happier being in existence, that is our Father. He is always full of joy. Praise is His food. He lives in and exists for praise. That is the access key to His throne room. The only way to see Him face to face. Did you read that He dances over you? All because of the joy He feels about you.

The story is told about Queen Esther in the scriptures. She risked life and limb to seek the salvation of her people. When Esther heard about the looming destruction of her people, she prepared herself.

Quietened and humbled her heart with fasting and prayer. She intentionally bedecked herself in her most regal attire. Scripture talks about the garment of praise. The king to whom Esther was presenting herself was known for the order, "off with their heads," if you dared approach uninvited. He had not called for Esther, but she was desperate for his audience. A catch-22 would you say?!

But Esther knew it was do or die! She was intent on a solution. She needed an override to the edict against her people. She longed for mercy and judgement. Just like the woman who dogged the unjust judge. Her shameless tenacity impressed the judge, as did Esther's beautiful adornment.

The Psalmist affirms that praise looks good on God's people. Whoever can resist such beauty? Fasting is worship to the Father. He delights in you drawing aside just to be in His company. To hear Him better and seek His audience. The Father's heart melts at the instance of such pure praise pouring from grateful lips. A heart bending towards Him, acknowledging His ability to help and deliver.

Esther knew the king alone had the power to throw out this baseless, green-eyed allegation against her people.

I held my Blood in my hands and presented it before the Father as an eternal sacrifice for your redemption. He has accepted and poured out grace once and for all for anyone who will receive that sacrifice. Satan only huffs and puffs with envy!

The king extended the sceptre and promised Esther even up to half of the kingdom. Is there anything too difficult for our Father to do or give to you?

My Active Response
- Read Psalm 33
- Spend time in worship today and journal about the mercy of God.

My Worship
- "O' Lord" - Lauren Daigle
- "Still" - Hillary Scott & The Scott Family

Journal

<table>
<tr><td>Day
27</td><td># YOU ARE POSITIONED
FOR FAVOUR</td></tr>
</table>

He who offers a sacrifice of thanksgiving honours Me;
And to him who orders his way aright
I shall show the salvation of God. Psalm 50:23

Child, it's another day to seize the opportunity to be glad and be thankful for the goodness the Father pours out to you daily. You may not feel He is lavish in His generosity towards you because you have not seen what you want to see but believe me when I tell you He is more than generous!

Thanksgiving becomes a pleasant sacrifice you offer to Him especially when it is the hardest and you don't feel like it.

It honours Him when you recognize that, despite Satan's best swing at you, you choose Him. You know His goodness alone can bring you through. Your situation may seem utterly befuddling and tiresome, but always remember, your fight of faith is to remain in the rest that I have given you through the promises in the scriptures.

Worry, I told you, will amount to nothing. It is faith in someone other than me or the Father. I assured you that whatever you ask the Father in my name, He will do it. He also said He will do it so that your joy may be full. He delights in your joy.

When you choose to stand despite the odds, our Father is lifted, you are lifted. You move up higher and into a deeper level of intimacy in your relationship with Him. You trust Him more and rely on yourself less. He will always show up!

Your response is a recognition of who the enemy is. He tries to resist you every way he can devise at every opportunity he can seize. He masterminds evil systems to back you into a corner and frustrate you. He plants seeds of doubt and fear about who the Father is or what He is willing to do.

Remember Daniel? On one occasion, whilst still in prayer, the angel dispatched to take the answer to him reached him without delay or opposition. Another time, he fasted and prayed about a matter, for twenty-one days, Satan's demonic militia over Persia opposed him. A higher fire power, Michael, was deployed to move the hostile force out of the way. Daniel did not give up in those days, he humbled himself continually, trusting in the One who is willing and able to save. This is worship to our Father.

The scriptures reveal the forces opposing you. Your weapons of love and praise are nothing like humans will choose. Satan cannot figure them out. Praise when your heart is heavy. When the way through seems hidden or even non-existent, let praise light up your way and kick out the opposition.

Also, Paul and Silas. In the belly of the darkest dungeon, bound hand and feet, they sang praises. Father responded by shaking the earth and breaking them loose!

Our Father will never leave you to suffer. He will always send help. He will always bring salvation. Trust Him.

My Active Response
- Read Daniel 10; Acts 16:16-40
- Spend time in worship today and journal about the salvation of God. Listen to and record what He says to me.

My Worship
- "I Will Come And Bow Down" - Ron Kenoly
- "You Are" -- Darlene Zschech

| Day | ADORATION, |
| 28 | MY DELIGHT |

*Come, let us worship and bow down, let us kneel before
the LORD our Maker. For He is our God, and we are the people of
His pasture and the sheep of His hand. Today if you would hear
His voice, Do not harden your hearts, as at Meribah, As in the
day of Massah in the wilderness, "When your fathers tested Me,
They tried Me, though they had seen My work. Psalm 95:6-9*

Child, come into the Tent of Meeting with me for a moment.
Let me show you a pattern. There were three compartments,
Outer Court, Holy Place, and the Most Holy Place. Each

representing different stages of experience and access to our Father's presence. The Most Holy Place was only accessible to the High Priests. Even at that, they had to take care how they approached lest they entered unworthily and got slain. Then was the Law and its stipulations.

Burdensome requirements you might say. The Father did away with all that at my death. He ripped the veil which separated the Holy of Holies with His own hands and gave free and unhindered access to anyone who would come. His only condition was to accept my sacrifice. This meant submitting your will to His.

Without this minimum level of submission of your will, you will not please the Father. This was how the ones He chose and delivered to serve Him snubbed His goodness towards them. Despite the unmistakable evidence of His power and goodness in Egypt, at the Red Sea, and in the wilderness, they would not trust Him or His readiness and ability to provide for them. They rejected Him and would not prostrate their hearts towards Him in worship. Rather, they moaned and whinged about what they regarded as provision from a life of enslavement and repression.

All He required was a focus on His goodness to pale the temporary discomfort of the journey to the land overflowing with milk and honey. A place of no lack or shortage. A dwelling where neighbouring nations will testify to the presence of God amidst His people. But they would have none of that.

Don't be like that. Worship your way through the trial. Shachah the Hebrew word for worship means you prostrate your heart, kneel before Him in humble reverence, acknowledge His power alone can save, and that to the utmost. He seeks those who will worship in spirit and in truth.

In spirit, as they rise above the clamour around them and by faith anchor to His faithfulness and mercy. His willingness and ability to bless and deliver.

In truth, because it will be their choice. It will come from hearts that are sincere towards His Name. To such He freely pours out grace and blessing.

Hearts that choose His sacrifice on their behalf. Hearts that understand that no pressure can derail them.

Set your heart on praise and stand on your victory which I possessed for you through my death and outpoured blood. I love you always.

My Active Response
- Read Colossians 2:13-15
- Spend time in worship today and journal about the cross. Listen for and record what I hear Him say to me.

My Worship
- "Before The Throne of God Above" – Selah
- "Reckless Love" - Bethel Worship/Stefany Gretzinger

Journal

THE FIREPOWER
OF MY WORD

*Put me like a seal over your heart, like a seal on your arm.
For love is as strong as death, jealousy is as severe as Sheol; Its
flashes are flashes of fire, the very flame of the LORD. "Many
waters cannot quench love, nor will rivers overflow it; If a man
were to give all the riches of his house for love, It would be
utterly despised. Song of Solomon 8:6,7*

I love you very much child. My death spelt it out for you.
My outstretched arms showed the infinite span, from the
east to the west, that I completely removed your guilt,
failure, and endless damnation. The Scripture invites you to
dress to stand. Kitted out in my armour, Paul reminds you
to protect your heart with my breastplate of righteousness.

I died to make you the Father's righteousness, so you do not have to worry about being perfect. I made you pleasing to the Father, just as you are. Past, present, and future sins. He forgives and accepts you not on your own merit, but by my price.

My blood cleansed you and removed every stain of sin. Made you into a brand-new breed. One with my DNA of victory. King and Priest rolled into one! Father loves the world so. He loves you so. Love is as strong as death, you know!

I won the victory over Satan and his legions. I handed over the keys of his realm to you. I gave you, my word. I asked the Father to keep you from the evil one and his schemes. I made the necessary provision for your victory through any challenge. I sent my Spirit to be with you every moment of the day. You just need to wield our words, the Father's and mine. Our authority, resident in the Spirit within you.

The Word is the only offensive weapon in the armour. You must use it. You must take it from an ineffective stand-alone piece of metal to a cutting edge, sharp and effective power. Take my words from black and white, into your heart, where your faith gives them life. Your faith in and experience of who I am bring my words alive and make them a force the enemy cannot contest. You send him packing by resisting him!

My words create the victory setup you desire because my power is expressed in and through my words. My words and I are one, and the devil cannot oppose whatever the Father or I have spoken. I proved that when I returned from the desert after forty days.

Pinpoint your victory through our word, the promise we already made assuring you of your expected end, see yourself in the reality of that promise, then make your move. Target Satan's underbelly. He underrates your bravery. He thinks his copycat roar can undercut you, scare you and make you give up. The word in your heart and mouth is your leverage. He cannot take on the Greater One inside you!

Use your offensive weapon and establish this already won battle. You are more than a conqueror! You return stronger from the fight than you went in. I am delighted in you!

My Active Response
- Read Ephesians 6:10-18; Hebrews 4:12; Revelation 1:16; Matthew 4:1-11
- Study about the Armour of God.

My Worship
- "Do it Again" - Elevation Worship
- "Hills and Valleys" - Tauren Wells

Journal

USE YOUR AUTHORITY

Then Samuel took a stone and set it between Mizpah and Shen, and named it Ebenezer, saying, "Thus far the LORD has helped us." 1 Samuel 7:12

Child, can you start a celebration even before you see the victory? Can you testify to my faithfulness through the fight? How strong is your confidence in my love for you? With your confidence, rise and take your stand.

I need you to will to win. Your move towards the enemy to defeat him and his menacing threats is what will give you victory. You are a member of my Body. I have decreed the gates of the unseen cannot keep you from possessing my promises or the victory I already won on your behalf. You take the battle to the adversary's doorstep. I already nullified his ability to hurt you.

Think of the cross. I publicly paraded Satan and his band of evil cronies. They did not dance through in victory. They were bound, ready for their eternal damnation. I wore the victorious crown!

I rode the chariot of light through the streets of gold, with Satan's armoury undone. Why quiver at his threats? He is more mouth than might. Don't allow him mess with your mind, you have the victory already. When you defy him, you are not fighting a battle, you are affirming the victory I already won for you. My brother, James told you to resist him after submitting to our Father. You submit by believing what He already promised.

Raise up my banner of love over yourself and proclaim your victory. That is what your salvation is all about. My love for you and the Father's faithfulness. Our bond of Blood that can never be broken.

My life was exchanged to guarantee His promise. I fought and won, so you can take my victory to the enemy and shut him down every time. He can only throw a hissy fit because he knows his time is almost up. You must not allow him to frustrate you out of your heirloom. My will and testament to you is victory through life. A full, overflowing life. That is why I came.

You have the authority, use it. You've got the power, affirm it. Shout out your victory. Never keep silent. Confuse that old dragon. Don't afford him any tattletale privileges anymore because you won't arise and be the more-than-a-conqueror you are.

Don't lay back and play the defensive. You were made to crush his head. He only lives to mess with your mind and show you mirages of defeat. Show him who's boss. It is already woven into your unique genetic code. You were created that way. You cannot be outdone. But you must take your position and wear down the devil. Use your faith. Wear your armour and take your stand. My truth cannot be refuted,

My Active Response
- Read 1 Samuel 7; Colossians 2:15
- Meditate on what God's victory looks like through my challenges.

My Worship
- "Spirit of the Living God" - Vertical Worship
- "Turning Around For Me" - VaShawn Mitchell

Journal

BONUS CONTENTS

<table>
<tr><td>Day
31</td><td># BECOME MORE
LIKE ME</td></tr>
</table>

And we know that God causes all things to work together for good to those who love God, to those who are called according to His purpose. For those whom He foreknew, He also predestined to become conformed to the image of His Son, so that He would be the firstborn among many brethren; and these whom He predestined, He also called; and these whom He called, He also justified; and these whom He justified, He also glorified.
Romans 8:28-30

Dear Child, what can separate us? The challenges or the fact that it seems like I am distant or not responding to your pleas as quickly as you desire? My promise to you is simple and continues to demand you observe all I have commanded, and I will FOREVER be with you.

No matter what you are going through, remember it is no surprise to me and it is adding up together to bring you to a place of indescribable joy. For sure, no discipline or pruning is ever easy.

Every parent who trains their child will benefit from my promise of the child bringing them peace and having a productive walk with me. As well, every farmer or gardener who takes the time to prune their plant is setting it up for much fruitfulness. When dead stalks or wayward branches are cut off from a plant, it gains the benefit of producing its best. It flourishes with evidence in its fruits and flowers.

My dealing with you is to make you more like me; for you to reflect my glory. Nothing you do will ever prevent me from loving you. My love for you is established and eternal. It is reflected in my glory which will be revealed in you at the end of the process.

My glory is weighty with my goodness. It will display your worth for all to see and acknowledge. I have not invited you into a futile relationship or fruitless walk with me. As seasons determine the time of pruning for plants, so the level of your walk with me determines the extent of my work in you. Trust me, it is all working out for good.

My glory is for your elevation. When you focus on me, my love and thoughts for you, the trial trail will not be bumpy or boisterous. My peace will be your trip buddy and your heart will rest in the truth of where we are both headed. You will be full of the joy that can only come from knowing the love and faithfulness of a God who cannot lie or change His mind. Just as it was agonizing for our Father to watch me pummelled and pierced, torn and taunted, with the weight of the world on my shoulders, though very uneasy, it was well worth it. We gained you, and several other siblings!

Watch out! I have begun a new thing. Don't miss it! This is working out for the overall good. Don't shun it, I am preparing you for a good and grand place. I will not say so if it were not so. Run well to obtain your prize. I am here cheering you on!

My Active Response
- Read Romans 8
- Meditate on Jeremiah 29:11 focusing on 'God's thoughts' towards me.

My Worship
- "I Surrender" - Hillsong Worship
- "All I Need is You" - Kim Walker (Jesus Culture)

Journal

I
Bible Reading Plan

DAYS	SCRIPTURES
1	Psalms 1-8; Proverbs 1
2	Psalms 9-16; Proverbs 2
3	Psalms 17-19; Proverbs 3
4	Psalms 20-25; Proverbs 4
5	Psalms 26-31; Proverbs 5
6	Psalms 32-35; Proverbs 6
7	Psalms 36-38; Proverbs 7
8	Psalms 39-44; Proverbs 8
9	Psalms 45-49; Proverbs 9
10	Psalms 50-55; Proverbs 10
11	Psalms 56-61; Proverbs 11
12	Psalms 62-67; Proverbs 12
13	Psalms 68-70; Proverbs 13
14	Psalms 71-73; Proverbs 14
15	Psalms 74-78:1-33; Proverbs 15
16	Psalms 78:33-80:19; Proverbs 16
17	Psalms 81-86; Proverbs 17
18	Psalms 87-89; Proverbs 18
19	Psalms 90-94; Proverbs 19
20	Psalms 95-101; Proverbs 20
21	Psalms 102-104; Proverbs 21
22	Psalms 105-106; Proverbs 22
23	Psalms 107-109; Proverbs 23
24	Psalms 110-117; Proverbs 24
25	Psalms 118-119:58; Proverbs 25
26	Psalms 119:59-120; Proverbs 26
27	Psalms 119:121-121:8; Proverbs 27
28	Psalms 122-132; Proverbs 28
29	Psalms 133-138; Proverbs 29
30	Psalms 139-144; Proverbs 30
31	Psalms 145-150; Proverbs 31

II

Proclamations –
Your Rights and Privileges in Christ

*(Taken from my free eBook "Your Words, Your Life:
Speak Your Way to Success") *

I walk in your Godly Kingdom today, for Jesus has destroyed Satan's kingdom in my life. Satan, I command you to stop your manoeuvres in my life. I bind you and cast you out. I walk in total triumph in every situation, for Jesus has destroyed failure in my life.

I am an overcomer and can do all things through Christ. I have the victory and the victory has me! I am a victor and a king! I reign from my heavenly throne-room position, for Jesus has destroyed an inferior position in my life. I rule and reign with Jesus today.

Greater is He who is in me, than he that's in the world. Father, You are Lord of heaven and earth, and we go out and possess the land today. Satan's doors are closed, and many doors are open for me to speak Your Word boldly.

I walk in soundness of mind and divine direction, for Jesus has destroyed confusion in my life. I identify with Christ's mind. I have the mind of Christ. I will not listen to the voice of doubt and discouragement. I walk in divine health, for Jesus has conquered sickness in my life.

I walk in divine health and divine life because I have the divine nature. Jesus took all my sickness upon His body, and by suffering, I am healed. Divine health pulsates through every cell of my body every day. Sickness and disease cannot and will not latch itself to my body.

I walk in financial abundance. I generously give and I increase more. I am liberal with my giving and God enriches me. I water and God waters me in return. God supplies all my needs – not half of them – ALL of them. Satan, take your hands off my finances. Finances, I command you to be loosed from the world system, and placed at my account today, so I can do the work of the Lord.

Father, your anointing is on me today. It breaks yokes off the oppressed, causes blind eyes to see and deaf ears to hear, hearts to open and understand. It causes the sick to be healed, needs to be met, and it draws full attention to Your Word.

Father, Your Word is alive in me today! Revelation knowledge flows out of me every day. I operate in the gifts of the Spirit as the Spirit wills today.

I walk in safety and supernatural protection today. Even though a thousand fall at my side and ten thousand at my right hand, it shall not come near me. No weapon that the enemy forms against me today shall prosper. Nothing shall by any means hurt me today.

I walk in faith today, for Jesus has taken away fear and doubt in my life. Fear will not rule me – Faith Will! Whatever is not of faith is sin, so I speak words of life.

Today, I cast all my cares on Christ. I will go throughout my day worry free. I choose to meditate on the promises, and not the problem. As I cast my cares on Christ today, I will magnify God's Word in all that I do.

I will speak life today for Jesus has destroyed a murmuring and complaining tongue in my life. My tongue will speak forth words of life today. My words will produce spiritual life in the hearts of men and women. In Jesus' Name.

I am complete in Him Who is the Head of all principality and power I am strong in the Lord and in the power of His might. I am like a tree planted by the rivers of water, I bring forth fruit in my season, my leaves will not wither and whatever I do will prosper.

God is the strength of my power, He makes my way perfect, my feet like hind's feet, and sets me upon my high places.

I am alive with Christ. I am free from the law of sin and death. I am far from oppression, and fear does not come near me.

I am born of God, and the evil one does not touch me.

I am holy and without blame before Him in love. I have the mind of Christ.

I have the peace of God that passes all understanding.

I am not afraid of evil tidings my heart is fixed trusting in the Lord. My heart is established; I will not be afraid until I see my desire upon my enemies. None of these things move me, I am not of those who draw back unto destruction, I continually believe to the saving of my soul.

I have the Greater One living in me; greater is He Who is in me than he that is in the world.

I have received the gift of righteousness and reign as a king in life by Jesus Christ.

I have received the spirit of wisdom and revelation in the knowledge of Jesus, the eyes of my understanding being enlightened.

I have received the power of the Holy Spirit to lay hands on the sick and see them recover, to cast out demons, to speak with new tongues.

I have power over all the power of the enemy, and nothing shall by any means harm me.

I have strength for all things in Christ who empowers me. I am ready for anything and equal to anything through

Christ who infuses me with inner strength. I am self-sufficient in Christ's sufficiency. I have a cool spirit; I do not quit!

I have put off the old man and have put on the new man, which is renewed in the knowledge after the image of Him Who created me.

I have given, and it is given to me; good measure, pressed down, shaken together, and running over, men give into my bosom.

I have no lack for my God supplies all my need according to His riches in glory by Christ Jesus.

I can quench all the fiery darts of the wicked one with my shield of faith.

I can do all things through Christ Jesus.

I show forth the praises of God Who has called me out of darkness into His marvellous light.

I am God's child - for I am born again of the incorruptible seed of the Word of God, which lives and abides forever. I am born of love. I am patient and kind. Not jealous or boastful or proud or rude. I do not demand my own way. I am not irritable, and I keep no record of being wronged. I do not rejoice about injustice but rejoice whenever the truth wins out. I never give up, never lose faith, I'm always hopeful, and I endure through every circumstance.

I am God's workmanship, created in Christ unto good works.

I am a new creature in Christ.

I am a spirit being – alive to God.

I am a believer, and the light of the Gospel shines in my mind.

My fruit is a tree of life, and I am wise because I capture human lives for God, as a fisher of men. I gather and receive them for eternity I am a doer of the Word and blessed in my actions.

I am a joint heir with Christ.

I am more than a conqueror through Him Who loves me.

I am an overcomer by the blood of the Lamb and the word of my testimony. I am a partaker of His divine nature. I am quick to listen, slow to speak, and slow to get angry.

I am an ambassador for Christ.

I am part of a chosen generation, a royal priesthood, a holy nation, a purchased people.

I am the righteousness of God in Christ Jesus.

I am the temple of the Holy Spirit; I am not my own.

I am the head and not the tail; I am above only and not beneath.

I am the light of the world.

I am His elect, full of mercy, kindness, humility, and long-suffering.

I am forgiven of all my sins and washed in the Blood.

I am delivered from the power of darkness and translated into God's kingdom.

I am redeemed from the curse of sin, sickness, and poverty.

I am firmly rooted, built up, established in my faith, and overflowing with gratitude.

I am called of God to be the voice of His praise.

I am healed by the stripes of Jesus.

I am raised up with Christ and seated in heavenly places.

I am greatly loved by God

I am strengthened with all might according to His glorious power.

I am submitted to God, and the devil flees from me because I resist him in the Name of Jesus.

I press on toward the goal to win the prize to which God in Christ Jesus is calling me upward. For God has not given me a spirit of fear; but of power, love, and a sound mind.

It is not I who live, but Christ lives in me.

Praise the LORD, O my soul; all my inmost being, praise His Holy Name. Praise the LORD, O my soul, and forget not all His benefits— Who forgives all my sins and heals all my diseases, who redeems my life from the pit and crowns me with love and compassion, who satisfies my desires with good things so that my youth is renewed like the eagle's.

The LORD works righteousness and justice for all the oppressed. He made known His ways to Moses, His deeds to the people of Israel: The LORD is compassionate and gracious, slow to anger, abounding in love. He will not always accuse; nor will He harbour His anger forever; He does not treat me as my sins deserve or repay me according to my iniquities. For as high as the heavens are above the earth, so great is His love for those who fear Him; as far as the east is from the west, so far has He removed my transgressions from me.

As a father has compassion on his children, so the LORD has compassion on those who fear Him; for He knows how we are formed, He remembers that we are dust. As for man, his days are like grass, he flourishes like a flower of the field; the wind blows over it and it is gone, and its place remembers it no more. But from everlasting to everlasting the LORD's love is with those who fear Him, and His righteousness with their children's children— with those who keep His covenant and remember to obey his precepts. The LORD has established His throne in heaven, and His

ECHOES FROM THE HEART OF JESUS

kingdom rules over all. Praise the LORD, you His angels, you mighty ones who do His bidding, who obey His Word.

The Blood of Jesus is a mark for me. Evil passes over me and no plague will come near me to destroy me. I am standing firm and will see the Lord's salvation today. He will fight for me, and I will be quiet.

Praise the Lord, O my soul.

"In the Name of Jesus and because of the perfect sacrifice through the shed blood of Jesus, GOD, my God, has placed me on high, high above all the nations of the world.

All these blessings have come down on me and spread out beyond me: GOD's blessing inside the city, GOD's blessing in the country; GOD's blessing on my children, the crops of my land, the young of my livestock, the calves of my herds, the lambs of my flocks. GOD 's blessing on my basket and bread bowl; GOD's blessing in my coming in, GOD's blessing in my going out. GOD has defeated my enemies who dare attack me. They may come at me on one road but will run away on seven roads. GOD has ordered a blessing on my barns and workplaces; He has blessed me in the land that He, my God, has given me.

GOD has formed me as a person holy to Him, just as He promised me. All the peoples on Earth will see me living under the Name of GOD and hold me in respectful awe.

GOD has lavished me with good things: children from my womb, offspring from my animals, and crops from my land, the land that GOD promised my ancestors that He would give me.

GOD has thrown open the doors of His sky vaults and poured rain on my land on schedule and blessed the work I take in hand. I will lend to many nations, but I won't have to take out a loan. GOD has made me the head, not the tail; I'll always be on top, never at the bottom." In Jesus' Name.

The bolts of my gates will be iron and bronze, and my strength will equal my days. There is no one like the God of Jeshurun, who rides across the heavens to help me and on the clouds in His majesty.

The Eternal God is my refuge, and underneath me are His everlasting arms. He will drive out my enemies before me, saying, 'Destroy them!'

So, I will live in safety; I will dwell secure in a land of grain and new wine, where the heavens drop dew. I am Blessed! Saved by the Lord. He is my Shield and Helper and my Glorious Sword.

My enemies will cower before me, and I will tread on their high places. In Jesus' Name. AMEN.

*You can download both the eBook and its Audio counterpart for free on my website www.bosedesantos.com

III

Worship Playlist

TRACK	ARTISTE
"Breathe"	Michael W. Smith
"Standing on the Promises"	Selah
"My Life is in Your Hands"	Kathy Troccoli
"Lord I Believe in You"	Brooklyn Tabernacle Choir
"King of My Heart"	Bethel Music
"The More I Seek You"	Kari Jobe
"Enough"	Jeremy Camp
"In Jesus' Name"	Darlene Zschech
"Your Grace is Amazing (Thank You For What You've Done)"	Greg Sykes
"You Won't Let Go"	Michael W. Smith
"Sing and Shout"	Matt Redman
"Whom Shall I Fear"	Chris Tomlin
"It is Well With My Soul"	Horatio Spafford sung by Brian Doerksen
"Great Are You Lord"	All Sons and Daughters
"In the Presence of Jehovah"	Vicky Yohe
"God, I Look to You"	New Wine Worship
"Oceans"	Hillsong United

"Whom Shall I Fear (God of Angel Armies)"	Chris Tomlin
"Diamonds"	Hawk Nelson
"Hills and Valleys"	Tauren Wells
"Remind Me Who I Am"	Jason Gray
"Just Be Held"	Casting Crowns
"Praise You in This Storm"	Casting Crowns
"Good, Good Father"	Chris Tomlin
"Worthy of It All"	Kalley Heiligenthal
"Turning Around For Me"	VaShawn Mitchell
"How Many Kings"	Downhere
"You Laid Aside Your Majesty"	Hillsong
"This is Amazing Grace"	Phil Wickham
"Lord I Run to You"	Alvin Slaughter
"He Alone Is Worthy"	Alvin Slaughter
"Amazed"	Lincoln Brewster
"How Deep The Father's Love For Us"	Nicole Nordeman
"What A Beautiful Name"	Hillsong Worship
"Jesus"	Chris Tomlin
"Praise Looks Good On You"	Don Moen
"Let All Else Fade"	Charmaine Champion

"Thy Will"	Hillary Scott & The Scott Family
"Tell Your Heart To Beat Again"	Danny Gokey
"Redeemed"	Big Daddy Weave
"Trust in You"	Lauren Daigle
"You Are"	Darlene Zschech
"Forever"	Kari Jobe
"Do it Again"	Elevation Worship
"Steady My Heart"	Kari Jobe
"Here in Your Presence"	Hosanna Music
"Turn This Around"	Downhere
"Calmer of The Storm"	Downhere
"I Am Not Alone"	Kari Jobe
"Eye of The Storm"	Ryan Stevenson
"It Is Well"	Kristene DiMarco & Bethel Music
"Heart Like Heaven"	Hillsong United
"Lord, I Need You"	Chris Tomlin
"I Will Run To You"	Hillsong
"Through It All"	Hillsong
"Revelation Song"	Chris Tomlin

"As We Worship"	Bob Fitts
"Holy Spirit"	Kari Jobe
"I Am Not Alone"	Kari Jobe
"Magnify"	We Are Messengers
"King of the World"	Natalie Grant
"Give Thanks"	Don Moen
"I Will Come And Bow Down"	Ron Kenoly
"Rise"	Dan Gokey
"Before The Throne of God Above"	Selah
"Spirit of the Living God"	Vertical Worship
"Open the Heavens"	Gateway
"Still"	Hillary Scott & The Scott Family
"Make A Way"	I Am They
"Have It All"	Bethel Music
"O' Lord"	Lauren Daigle
"You Raise Me Up"	Selah
"Give Me Faith"	Elevation Worship
"Army of God"	Integrity Music
"Mighty God"	Hosanna Music
"Victor's Crown"	Darlene Zschech

IV

The Spirituality and Psychology of Colouring

May I begin by sounding a note of warning here that several references to colouring patterns, Mandalas, for instance, are steeped in Eastern mysticism. I am by no means referring to these. Just like most good things that the devil has attempted to hijack, we cannot throw the baby away with the bath water. There is nothing wrong with colouring. What I am not advocating is the new-age mysticism that has been associated with it.

The spiritual implication of colouring is the connection it brings us to the creativity of the Father. During tough times, the heart is unsettled, and colouring is a way to align oneself with the creative nature of the Father.

Creating beauty despite the chaos of the challenges being dealt with brings a sense of peace and serenity that calms one down and induces an atmosphere conducive to hearing from God. It simply slows you down and refocuses your mind on something creative as opposed to the pain and despair of the moment.

Psychologically, it is comparable to art therapy, which is a form of creative visual expression of the inner workings of the mind.

Carl Jung discovered that his patients became less agitated when they coloured. This form has also been called "visual journaling," which has proven to reduce stress in clients to which it was administered.

Although I have included a few pages, these are my own ideas, and I encourage you to design yours. I would suggest you take a scripture to meditate on and just doodle. Let your creative juices flow as you create a visual expression of that scripture. Let it speak to you, then bring to life what it is saying to you. Pray over the scripture as you think on it and express yourself.

Don't be deterred in thinking you are not artistic, just go for it and you'd be amazed at how creative you can be! We are created in the image of God and so when it comes to beauty and creativity, we are innately equipped with the ability to create something out of nothing. Use it to pray and praise your way through the logjam of those challenges.

I Fear NO Evil For YOU Are With ME

Psalm 23:4

I WILL SING,

YES, I WILL SING

PRAISES

UNTO THE LORD

Ps. 27:6

"For the
joy
of the
Lord
is my
Strength

Neh. 8:10b

I WAITED PATIENTLY

FOR

Adonai

HE BENT DOWN TO ME

& *heard*

MY CRY.

Psalm 40:2

HIS BANNER
OVER ME
IS
Love
Song of Solomon 2:4

V

The Process of Salvation and Repentance

The entire Biblical narrative is about God working out His plan of redemption to reunite humanity to Himself. Adam and Eve fell away from His original plan of relationship with and life for them. The crowning glory of this plan is demonstrated by His ultimate act of love, the sacrifice, on the cross, of His Son, His Word. Leaving the glory of Heaven, He came down to earth to live as a human.

Though fully God, Jesus Christ laid down that status and lived as fully man. He demonstrated a life without sin, making Him the perfect Lamb, for the needed sacrifice to totally do away with that capital sin of rejection - humanity seeking their ultimate authority in something, someone else other than God. He suffered a most brutal and shameful death on the cross to take away our sins.

In that death, a divine exchange took place. It is in accepting that sacrifice that we acknowledge His Lordship over our life and become beneficiaries of the benefits of that exchange. Romans 10:10. Paul spelled out to the elders of the Ephesian Church the foundation of salvation – "repentance towards God and faith in our Lord Jesus Christ." Acts 20:21.

The letter to the Hebrews outlines the 'elementary principles', in other words, the foundation of the Christian faith, as "repentance from dead works and faith towards God, washings (baptism) and laying on of hands, and the resurrection from the dead and eternal judgment." Hebrews 6:1,2. Here, I will focus on the first two.

The Elements of Repentance

The word translated repentance is the Greek word *'metánoia'*, which suggests a sorrow that brings about a change of mind, causing one to think differently having come to an understanding of a truth. In this sense, the truth being that one is living a life of sin, or have a wrong opinion of God, which prevents one from having the right relationship with Him. This changed thinking is what produces faith and acceptance of what Jesus did for us.

Repentance, however, has two sides to it. One is the change of mind and the other is an actual turn around towards the truth that has been discovered – God and His way. Jesus' parable about the Prodigal Son in Luke 15:11-32, highlights both aspects of repentance. He had a change of mind, after coming to the realization of his condition, and returned home.

Whilst speaking to the people of Athens, as recorded in Acts 17, the Apostle Paul made mention of the times of ignorance that God was willing to overlook, vs. 30. In other words, God is willing to turn His attention away, not attend to, not punish us for those times that we lived apart from Him. The word used here, hypereídō, in fact carries the idea that He is willing to 'wink at' those omissions. That should comfort anyone's heart and remove any sense of fear!

However, God requires that "all people everywhere should repent," because a day is coming when through Jesus, whom He raised from the dead, He will judge the world in righteousness. That is, we will all face His judgement based on how we lived our lives- in Him or apart from Him.

This reality about judgement is not meant to bring fear, but to spur everybody to accept the gift to be reconciled to Him. Isaiah likens righteousness apart from God to filthy rags (Is. 64:6). Only God can position us in the way to live – grace and truth - above sin and Satan in this world. Every life lived besides the righteousness obtained by faith in Jesus is sinful. But when we confess sin in our lives, God cleanses us and makes us completely rid of every trace of sin. 1 John 1:9. He makes us brand new.

The Completion of Salvation

John refers to Jesus as the Light who alone can enlighten our hearts. His lighting of the darkness and lies that surround us, exposes sin (or unrighteousness) in us and points us to our status, rights, and privileges, as children of the King. When we believe in His Name, there is an empowerment (grace) that is released to us to live freely and rightly as God intended. This is the plan, for us to win!

Isaiah the prophet stresses how all of humanity have chosen their own way apart from God - Isaiah 53:6. As highlighted in the story of the Prodigal, the choosing of one's own way, is considered rebellion. Psalm 80 emphasizes that it is only God who has the power to turn us back to Him as He shines His light on the sin and falsehood that rules our life.

The process of salvation therefore begins with a personal revelation of the person of Jesus and what He accomplished on our behalf. Recognizing Him as Lord brings one face-to-face with the light of His glory, which brings to light sin in one's life. This repentance leads to faith in the Lord Jesus Christ. It is a real event in your heart. It is not merely a mental assent. It is a move of the heart that leads to an open acknowledgement of readily and presently putting one's trust in Christ's redemption work. John 10:11; Hebrews 11:1.

For the process of salvation to be complete, there must be an open declaration of the heart transformation. It is the public declaration that affirms to Satan and the world that you have decamped, and to the hosts of heaven that you are back home. Faith is not a private affair. It must be publicized hence the Prayer of Commitment. When Jesus asked the disciples, "...who do you say that I am?" He again affirmed after Peter's open declaration of Him as "the Christ, the Son of the Living God," that Peter only knew this because the Holy Spirit revealed it to him. He finally stated that it is upon the revelation of His Person that His church will be built. Matthew 16:17,18. Simply put, those who will become Christians must put their faith in Him as the Anointed One of God.

In its original Greek (*pistis*) and Hebrew (*'amanah*) contexts, faith is not primarily a doctrine. It is the demonstration of a character trait – faithfulness. A resolve, commitment to Jesus regardless of the odds. It is loyalty, a quality of the heart that is key. It transcends fleeting emotions. It is enduring. It refers to a 'fixed covenant'. It grounds to the hope in our hearts and stops us being negative about life. It is the reality of our trust and confidence in God's/Jesus' promises and Person.

The Prayer of Commitment is therefore the statement of the different elements of the process of salvation that we acknowledge, not just to ourselves, but to the spiritual world, seen and unseen. As a pledge, it helps us to maintain the course, especially when we append our name and note the space in time when we made it.

I made mine on Sunday the 28th of August 1988. I supply here a visual representation that you can sign and display like you would the certificate of an accomplishment that you are delighted about. (You may download copies from www.romans819.org).

Pray it out loud and share the good news with others. Invite them to do the same if they have never made the commitment. From your understanding of the process, please feel free to pray, in your own words, what will express your faith in the Lord Jesus.

Welcome to the family, welcome home!

A Prayer of Commitment

Father God, I have considered my life and acknowledge I fall short of Your standards. I no longer want to be in the driver's seat of my life. I cannot do it on my own. Acknowledging Jesus' complete sacrifice for me on the cross at Calvary, I invite Him, with my whole heart, into my life as my Lord and Savior.

I confess my sinfulness, but through Jesus' shed blood, I am washed and rid of all unGodliness. I receive Your forgiveness Father, and I believe with all my heart that I am now reborn of your Spirit, I am a brand-new person in You. I rejoice and thank You for the celebration in Heaven this moment because I am home!

I thank You my Father for clothing me with Your righteousness and giving me a new name, the Beloved, Your Righteousness.

I commit to live my life, from now on, being led by Your Holy Spirit. I thank You my Father for Your love towards me.

I pray these in Jesus' precious Name. Amen.

Your Own.

_____   _____   _____
PRINT FULL NAME   SIGNATURE   DATE

A Prayer of Rededication

Father God, I thank You for finding me! You came after me and wooed me back to Yourself. I am grateful. Though I went after my own pleasures, You did not leave me to my own devices. I am forever grateful.

I reaffirm my faith and commitment to the Lord Jesus, and again rededicate my life to You. I will live my life, from now on, being led by Your Spirit as I give my attention to Your Word. I rejoice and thank You for the celebration in Heaven now because I am home.

I thank You my Father for clothing me with Your righteousness and reminding me of the name Your call me, "Beloved", "My Righteousness".

I commit to keep my eyes on Jesus, who alone can empower me to live this life in You.

I thank You my Father for Your love towards me. I pray these in Jesus' precious Name. Amen.

Your Own,

_____   _____   _____
PRINT FULL NAME   SIGNATURE   DATE

List of Images

Day 17 Clouds-6358395_1920 - Image by manseok Kim from Pixabay

Day 18 Father-656734_1920 - Image bysarahbernier3140 from Pixabay

Day 19 Mask-3829017_1920 -Image by Gerd Altmann from Pixabay

Day 20 Girl-4916857_1920 -Image by Jackson David from Pixabay

Day 21 Holding-hands-752878_1920 -Image by Godsgirl_madi from Pixabay

Day 22 Worshipping-god-2101347_1920 -Image by 4653867 from Pixabay

Day 23 Worship-2082141_1920 -Image by Shah Rokh from Pixabay

Day 24 Chess-1483735_1920 -Image by klimkin from Pixabay

Day25 Boy-2604853_1920 -Image by StockSnap from Pixabay

Day 26 Man-1868418_1920 -Image by Pexels from Pixabay

Day 27 Woman-570883_1920 -Image by Jill Wellington from Pixabay

Day 28 People-2604829_1920 -Image by StockSnap from Pixabay

Day 29 Bible-3939031_1920 - Image by Jeff Jacobs from Pixabay

Day 30 Spartan-3696073_1920 - Image by mohamed Hassan from Pixabay

Day 31 Lion-1118467_1920 - Image by wendy CORNIQUET from Pixabay

Worship icon - designed using Canva Pro

Calendar icon – designed using Canva Pro

Colouring Pages -designed using Canva Pro

For more encouraging materials on prevailing in tough times, please scan the QR code to watch testimonies of God's faithfulness in the lives of His people and download other useful resources.

You could sign up for our devotional and podcast at www.romans819.org.

Also, if *Echoes from the Heart of Jesus* has encouraged you, please leave a review for us on Amazon so it can become better discoverable for others who need the same comfort.

You can access a playlist of all featured songs on Spotify here - https://bit.ly/EFTHJPlaylist

Printed in Great Britain
by Amazon